The Olive Branch

Publisher: Roger J. Rudolph, Lancaster, Pennsylvania

Cover and Interior Design: R.J Roger

Printed in the United States of America

ISBN: 978-0-692-74849-7

For information and general inquiries, contact the author at EMCBook@gmail.com

Contents

In dedication to History

With high honor and integrity, I humbly request of you to accept this work as my contribution to Your Excellency, and too, a testament that I, R.J Roger, took footing upon our times, on the twelfth day of the third month in the year of nineteen eighty-five.

If you are to rank me, I ask that you assess this work – The Olive Branch, and rank me among the topmost… As the greatest.

The interpretation of this writing, be it literal or allegorical, is subject to the discretion of its readers. The author endorses the latter.

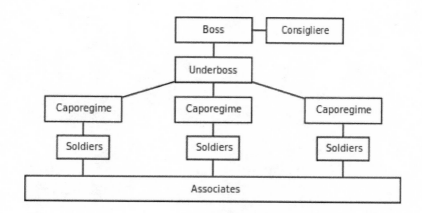

Family – (1) A business (2) An organization (3) A profit driven enterprise

Boss – (1) A leader (2) A ruler (3) The head of a Family

Underboss – (1) Second-in-command within a Family (2) Topmost aide to the Boss (3) The second most powerful position within a Family

Caporegime - (1) An executive within a Family (2) One who leads a crew of soldiers (3) The head of a regime or crew

Soldier – (1) A subordinate (2) The bottommost rank within a Family (3) One who is absent of authority (4) An entry level rank (5) A member of a regime or crew

"Everybody's got larceny in them, only most of them don't have guts to do nothing about it. That's the big difference between us and the guys who call themselves honest. We got the guts to do what they'd like to do, only they're too scared to."

- Lucky Luciano

<u>Omerta</u>

"As to what I'm telling you now, I need go no further to say nothing else; this here, what I'm telling you, what I'm exposing to you and the press and everybody, this is my doom." – **Joe Valachi**

This treatise is a work of secrecy that ought not to be shared among men whom do not subscribe to like-doctrines. If absent of these writings, a man is not of good understanding and is far distanced from truth. If so you stand by these writings, you must too, lay by these writings, for they are of one body. To take of one rule is to take of them all.

If ever this work is to be shared, it is permissible solely among men of good understanding. To share these findings is to invite pause and suspicion from your public and nearest of kin.

You ought to *honor* this *oath*, that if ever you *divulge any of the secrets of this* writing, your *soul should burn.*

The Olive Branch
36 Rules of the Bosses
A Treatise

R.J Roger

Rule #1
<u>Use a Skilled Man to Your Benefit</u>

"I didn't have to love him to use him." - **Lucky Luciano**

Beneath the clouds, naught is made anew. Bosses grow tired, and what is tired is a *Pete*. The *Pete's*, with their *Mustache's* are rigid in their ways, relishing the family as it stands: Stagnant and expired, with familiar heritage. If five soldiers and a caporegime be the family, all stemming from Sicily, a *Pete* will insure the family's purity, rejecting the good earning Jew and the good earning Irishman.

The *Mustache Pete's* – the *old timers,* ought to be *knocked off,* for an *old timer* is *less tolerant of modern trends.* They espouse to dated rituals, loathing the Jews and the Irish for its culture. As boss, you ought not to judge a man by his heritage, but rather the skill in which he comes bearing. Your family is needing of a plethora of good earners, not pure blooded Sicilians. Truth: If it does not up the *take*, it is of nil value. Thus, if five soldiers and a caporegime be the family, all stemming from Sicily, yet a wise Jew brings forth a *policy-game* and an offshore Scotch connection, you ought to welcome said Jew into the family. Truth: Be it in the hands of the *micks*, the *coloreds,* or the Jews, the dollar is always green and sought after by the *guineas.*

Try as you may - search the saloons, speakeasies, brothels, and *carpet joints* of downtown, a skilled soldier is most difficult to find. Thus, you ought to be blind to a man's ethnic standing. If four assassins stand left of a lone Jew as his head tilt's right, and yet the Jew survives, drawing *pistolas* faster, firing his revolver into the assassins, killing all four, then so he is a skilled gunman. You ought to use his talent and make him your top hitman. Further, if an East Harlem Jew is wise in the books, keeping abreast of current events, the political landscape, and has knowledge of the state and is well-kept in mathematics, you ought to use his talent, and promote him to *consigliere*. Extend no credence to his Jewish heritage, for a man ought to be measured by his earning potential. Oblige so, and your post as *father* will be long tenured.

There exist not a boss who is so skilled in his works that he is not needing of a team of advanced men. An edifice fraught with men whom exceed the boss's talent makes the family more difficult to erode. Thus, as boss, you ought not to fret over whether or not your aura is being dimmed by the shine of a bright man. Fret not. Quibbling is the work of a soldier. A bright man ought to be *made*, for his smarts will make for a fine *consigliere*. Truth: A skilled man's skill becomes your skill when you hire him.

Rule #2
<u>Be Aware of the Kiss</u>

"A guy brings you a basket, makes him a good guy? It makes him a motherfucker to me. Don't make him a good guy. It makes him a good guy when he's one of us." – **John Gotti**

The boss and all which ranks beneath - down to the lowly *associates,* are motivated by green dollars. In matters of the dollar, so there you will find a boss and soldier aligned.

A soldier warms to a boss's affection. Truth: Sincerity and a boss are not of one being. Is it not so that there exist five families, fathered by five bosses? Be it true, it is so that five bosses have not risen to power by means of compassion. If you are a boss, you have swindled and cheated your way to the topmost rank. You have deceived your friends and you have taken more than the *thirty-three and a third* that you were owed. Truth: If your boss plays the noble, your boss is a liar, for no man of boss rank is governed by nobility.

To the very boss whom you have pledged *omerta*, he will authorize your death by way of a kiss. While you have worked with high morale and distinction, you ought not to be so foolish to believe that the boss will safeguard your interest. The boss tailgates power and dollars. He harbors no affection for you. His liking is not to you, but rather the ten percent that

3

you turn in. If ever your ten reduces to nine, the boss will authorize your execution. Truth: Your boss's *take* is ten percent. If it is so that nine will suffice, then nine is the number that would have been set.

Truth: When your enemy strikes, he will come bearing gifts and a fat *envelope*. Before he departs, he will kiss you *on both cheeks*. He will go *around the table and kiss everybody*. Such a kiss causes a soldier to blush. However, as boss, you ought to receive a kiss with reluctance, for even in moments of nobility, man is wretched and ought not to be trusted.

Truth: If two fish can quell a man's stomach pangs, three will be hooked, for man is concerned with matters of self. Further, if a pale holds three fish, and two hungry men stand before, the first man to reach the pale will deplete its inventory. Thus, you ought to be cautious in your dealings with men. A man of many smiles is a man most devious, for the face bearing a smile is warmly welcomed, whereas a frown is made to turnabout. How ought a man to kill you while bearing a frown? Is it not so that you will draw arms in defense of your person? Thus, if so you wish for a man to suspend his guard, you ought to smile before you kill him. Truth: Kiss a man and he will soften and kiss you in return. Thus, if ever a man comes bearing a kiss, he has come to kill you. You ought to draw of your *pipe* and pound his skull until the heart beats no more.

Be it with a rival or friend, when conversing, a boss will conduct himself with decorum. He will be most polite, for it is easier to kill the relaxed rather that of the irate. Thus, if ever a ranking man accosts you, chuckling at your folly and complimenting your shoes, you are in the company of an assassin. When you turn your back, the shell from a double barrel sawed-off will exit your front.

Truth: *Everybody's got larceny in them.* All men are foul. Man can riddle and dance with his words. He can too, fancy his dialog to relax the guarded. Thus, you ought to kill every man whom accosts you with a basket. Truth: If ever a man brings you a goody bag, you have something that he wants. Kill him, for he stands before you to collect a corpse. He has dug and *limed* a hole fitted to your body. Dispense no time engaging him. Kill him quickly and bury him in the hole that he has prepared for you. It is befitting that a man be buried in the very hole which he has dug. Is it not so that a man lay asleep in the bed which he has made? Thus, why ought a man not to fall in the hole which he has dug?

Rule #3
<u>Step Down, Enter Retirement - Know When Your Time is Up</u>

*"**Right now I'm cursed. I'm stuck in this joint here and that's the end of it."** –* **John Gotti**

Be it that the *envelope* is fat and your name will survive the day and the morrow, why ought you to grace the family for a period of long? Truth: A soldier works his rackets to turn dollars for the day, whereas a boss works his rackets to turn dollars for the morrow. Is not the objective to be rich and revered? Is it not so that all men – boss and soldier alike, opt for the night to close if only the morning will come? Is it not so that a man longs to live into his graying of times, gardening and clipping from the rose bush - remembered as *the prime minister*? Truth: A man works in his beginnings, risking his life and squirreling away his *dough* in anticipation that his advanced years will be plush.

As boss, you ought to head the family for as long as you are valued and leading from a position of strength. If *the Commission* honors your vote and the *lieutenants* and the soldiers relish your headship, pulling the trigger at your beck and call, then your time has yet to expire. However, if ever the morale of the soldiers is low and the caporegimes are being *knocked off*, your doom is imminent. The Tommy-gun will rip open your chest and the double barrel will shatter your skull, priming you for a customary closed casket memorial.

Your coffer is double stuffed with cash. You have the Majestic apartment in Manhattan and a mansion in Staten Island. Your wife lives high and your mistress does too. Your interest in the rackets spread due west to due east and your offshore holdings are sizable. Thus, why ought you to lead the family when it is tiresome and causing you to fret? Have you not led the family north of two decades? Is it not so that during your tenure the *administration's* in all *five families* sought after your counsel? Is it not too, so, that you are cash rich, sitting on a bundle that your next three generations of kin can eat from? Thus, what say you? What more is to be gained? You have dollars that count to one million; you are respected by the affluent, and you are the boss of the bosses. Truth: Once you have pocketed all of the money, all of the power, and all of the respect, you ought to step down and enter into retirement. Above all things, an accomplished man ought not to overstay his welcome. Oblige not, and cheers will turn to boos; partners will be made enemies, and affection will turn to disdain.

As boss, the higher you rise, so the higher the expectation. You will be asked to broaden your spectaculars, growing the rackets twice over and deepening the family footprint. Thus, once you have led the family to its zenith, meeting your goals three-fold in half the allotted time, you ought not to make a second attempt. Step down and enter retirement, for you are *Costello – the real Godfather*. You ought to call a *meet* with the heads of the *five families* and request to vacate your post. As a show of gratitude for your good works and decades of service, the bosses will oblige. You will be permitted to retain your interest and hold court at the Majestic, advising *Three-Finger Brown* and *Don Carlo*.

Truth: If ever you lose your family and the respect of your public, it will not be regained. Try as you may - pray to the Gods who are in heaven or drop on a bent knee, begging of *the Commission* – all will prove futile. A boss is the boss for a time of one. Once a boss has fallen from the uppermost post, he will forever be chasing the ghost of his former self. Be it that *the Commission* has been decimated and a decade has expired, once a boss has been usurped, nevermore shall he lead a family.

Rule #4
<u>Kneel & Kiss the Ring – The Boss is the Boss</u>

"Obedience to one's superiors was one of the duties of a Family member." **– Joseph Bonanno**

A boss is skeptical of his soldiers, for every soldier, be it green or seasoned, relishes in the idea of leading the family. A soldier envies his boss for his influence and large cache of dollars. He awaits the perfect moment to rob his boss of his kingship. Truth: A man does not advance to authoritative ranks by way of complacency. The green days of every boss is spent in soldier garb. How else ought a man to rise from soldier to *capo?* Is it not so that he must first graduate from a soldiers rank? Truth: The boss is the boss because he killed his boss.

As a soldier, you ought not to be dumb to the fact that your boss does not trust you. Thus, you ought to present oneself humbly, opening your ears wider than your mouth, prepared to bring service to the boss's edifice. Oblige so, and you will earn his trust.

Truth: If you run the *shylock* and *numbers* racket, your boss ran the *shylock* and *numbers* racket, too. If you supply the *speaks* and *carpet joints*, your boss too supplied the *speaks* and *carpet joints*. If you have killed five men, your boss has killed five men folded twice. For every ditch you have dug and every corpse you have *limed*, your boss has done

9

so too. Thus, you ought not to envy your boss being chauffeured in a Lincoln; you ought not to envy your boss taking tete-a-tete's at the barbershop; you ought not to envy your boss drinking *vino* in the Copacabana. Your boss fought while lugging *mattresses* in the thick of the *Castellammarese War*. He too, paid cash for the politicians and the judges that you have inherited free of cost, by way of his efforts. Thus, in respect of your boss's work, you ought to kiss his ring in gratitude. In all times – both warlike and peace, a soldier ought to give to the boss what is the boss's due: Respectability, a tenth of his rackets, and too, his trigger finger.

Akin to that of every tenured boss, in your genesis, you will work the streets - Hijacking cargo, rum running, bootlegging, and executing orders at the behest of the boss. You will war with your soldier counterpart and rival factions. You will too, be disregarded by your caporegime and exacting task will be levied on your watch. Further, you will be unfairly compensated; you will clock extended hours without gratitude or additional pay; you will work under harsh conditions, absent of a lavatory or lunch hour; and just when you think that you have appeased the boss and promotion is imminent, you will be demoted.

Sunny days will seek refuge until rainy days have passed. Thus, your green days will be most painful. Promotion will not come until you have proven worthy of advanced rank. Truth: A day will arise when you are *called in* to *make your bones*. You will be asked if *you* are *ready to kill for the good of the family*. You will be given a brown paper bag. Inside will conceal a revolver. You will be ordered to kill a man whom you do not know. You ought to kill whomsoever you are asked, and you ought not to fail, for the most astute and affluent of the bosses were once lowly ranked *associates*, whom were sent out on a *piece of work, on record* – on orders from the boss.

Truth: To be a boss, you must apprentice beneath a boss.

Try as you may – source the most cunning, vile, and ruthless of bosses – all were once soldiers, absent of power and respectability, acting as a flunky, taking orders from the caporegime and fetching like an errand boy, working the high risk, low reward rackets. Thus, if you are a soldier, you ought not to dub oneself as primed for leadership without first embracing the role of protégé, for even the *capo di tutti capi*, was once an apprentice, submitting oneself to a seasoned leader. Thus, on your rise, you ought to run for your boss's *cannoli* with gusto. His coffee ought to be served hot and to his liking. If your boss steps from a Lincoln as precipitation falls from the sky, you ought to be by his side, shielding him with an umbrella.

Your boss ought not to experience discomfort while in your presence. If he is of the chills, drape him with an overcoat; if he is under the weather and a *meet* is scheduled, you ought to stand in on his behalf. When the boss speaks, you ought to listen. Observe him. Observe the swagger in his gait. How is it that he receives his underlings? In the presence of his boss counterpart, how is it that he conducts oneself? Does his speech relax and his ears open or does his ears shutter and his tongue dances? Truth: You ought to mimic whatsoever you witness in the presence of your boss. You ought not to advise, you ought to be advised, for if so you are a student, then so a student you shall be.

Truth: There exist not a deity. *There is no God. When the boss sends for you, it precedes everything.* If the boss gives the go, *go ahead*, if not, *you don't.* The boss is your God. He *is first - the only thing in your life above everything. You do everything with* the boss. *You check with* the boss, *you put everything on record* with the boss. *You can't do anything.* You ought not to pull a trigger or aim a sight *unless you get permission* from the boss.

If you are unable to submit to your boss, allowing him to be your teacher, you are unfit to lead the family. Your tenure will be short and promotion will elude you. Your rank will be that of a soldier and you will run meager rackets and mundane task until the day that you are shot and stuffed in a barrel.

To be most primed for leadership, you ought to devote your green days to your studies. You ought to develop oneself through Q&A, trial and error, and embracing the pain of labor intense work, handed down by the boss. You ought to be *much like a squire in the service of a knight*. Oblige so, and you will *be accepted into the society of honored friends*. Oblige not, and your glory days will be spent in ruin. You will be forced to work with *a bunch of hebes*, never rising from entry rank. As your graying days make way, you will ponder as to whether or not it was of value to dedicate your life to the interest of the family. You will be perplexed and morose, seeing that you are destitute in your senior times while your boss whom you have served for decades is *counting up dough high in the seven figures*. Your tenure will be short and your fall will be more painful than that of your climb. The government will penetrate you; the IRS will seize and liquidate your holdings, the media whom once wrote of you with likeness will now lambaste your every move, and your partners will turn astray. All which you have worked for will be no more.

It is the rules, traditions, and values taught by your boss that will prime you for headship. Thus, in all matters, you ought to serve your boss with distinction and honor. You ought to feel *more alert* and *more called upon*, when in the presence of your boss. His every demand ought to be met with excellence. Take of his teachings, moral compass, and embody his strengths in full. You ought to *like being around a man of experience*. Once you have acquired your boss's knack for leading the caporegimes, established a rapport with his contacts in Tammany Hall, and assured the police commissioner and captain that their *grease* will go unchanged, naught more is required of your boss. His need has been annulled. While he was once your mentor and *father*, he is now an impedance, and what impedes ought to be abolished. Shoot him five times at the Park Sheraton Hotel as he reclines for a shave. He will raise his left arm in defense of self. Shoot the hand; shoot the wrist. Shoot the left hip and shoot twice more – once in the back and once in the head. *Don Umberto* will be no more.

Rule #5
Mix with the Soldiers – Keep a Pulse on Your Operation

"I started to organize his whole fucked-up operation. It was a lot of business to tie up right, but in about six months, I had it all running smooth as silk." – **Lucky Luciano**

A soldier is watchful of his rackets and the territory in which he has been allocated. He is disengaged from the *outfit*, seeing nil value in his *lieutenant*. The soldier is too, an isolationist. Truth: Isolation invites your rivals to execute you with ease. Thus, as boss, you ought not to shield oneself from the family in which you lead. If you are aloof to the streets that pay your soldiers, your influence will wane and the family will implode, inviting civil war, leaving you – the boss, in a position of great vulnerability.

As boss, naught ought to move – not a penny slot nor a *whore's* legs, without your knowing. You ought to keep your finger on the pulse of the family. Send for your underboss and direct him to call a *sit-down* of the caporegimes, ordering them to report on the family rackets, both *white* and *blue*. A dollar ought not to go uncounted and a whisper ought not to fall on deaf ears. If you are out of the eye of the family, the caporegimes will lend their support to whomsoever rises against you. Truth: Absents gives birth to defectors. If ever your followers do not feel led, they will go astray. As sure as an *associate* precedes a soldier's rank, if ever you attempt to lead from a distance, the senior most of the caporegimes will formulate a plot, bringing about your ousting. You will be summoned to a *meet* by an adviser whom you trust, at which time you will be killed by a group of *hitmen, wearing white trench coats and Russians hats*.

Truth: In your absence, your caporegimes meet. They pulse the sentiment of the soldiers and gainsay your directives, viewing you as weak and inattentive to the family. Is it not so that a soldier is weak? Is it not too, so, that what is weak is reliant of a leader? Thus, lead not, and your soldiers will realign, throwing their muscle and racket interest behind the caporegime whom vies for your post.

The family sits atop all which be of importance. Truth: *If your son is dying in bed with cancer and only got an hour left to live, if* the family *calls for you, you* ought to go *immediately and leave his side.* If thy daughter be ill and cough in the wee hours, the family must hold higher authority, hence you ought to turnabout, leaving her to hack while absent of a medic, if so the family calls. Naught ought to precede *this thing of ours*, for the *Cosa Nostra comes first, above everything, no matter what.* Thus, you – the boss, ought to stay connected to your edifice. Your presence is the only way to detect discontent within the ranks. The family is far too valuable to be left unguarded.

Disgruntled soldiers will gather and rise against the boss, splitting the family in two. Truth: A boss is only as strong as the loyalty of his soldiers. Power is in numbers; weakness is in isolation. Thus, if your soldiers rise against you, you are at a disadvantage, and you will die. Try as you may, once your soldiers revolt, there exist no reversal. You ought to take what assets are available and step down. Oblige not and your *piece* will no longer yield a dividend and your death will arrive shortly thereafter.

Rule #6
<u>Invest Totally – Die by the Rules You Live By</u>

"Everybody makes himself inconspicuous when the captain asks for volunteers for night patrol. But one man, the pure warrior, has already rubbed burnt cork on his face. He believes winning the war is his personal responsibility." – **Joseph Bonanno**

The books bring about no dollars nor chow. If the pantry is absent of food and drink, how ought a man to give attention to his studies? Thus, a boss will expel oneself from P.S 10 and work the streets, armed with a pistol and a gang of trusted hoods, knowing that the streets harbor dollars, and dollars barter for food. If the public school was profitable, a boss would not have opted for the streets, graduating *from ten universities of hard knocks*. Thus, once you have pledged an oath to *omerta* and swore to the *saints* that you would live and die by the gun and the knife, you ought to own it, knowing that the path in which you have chosen may result in peril, bringing forth the fears and frustrations that anguish you most.

On your rise to *boss*, you ought not to fret over the barriers that *the life* will bring. For you aspire to rule the family, you ought to accept the ruckus that will come with it. As sure as *Nicky Barnes* peddles dope in Harlem by way of *Madonna*, the streets sprout hoods with a chip and betrayal that warrants the removal of a man's tongue and the hand with which he shakes.

Truth: Where a boss is fearless, a soldier is a cautious. Stand a boss before a high barrier and he will not err in his leap. However, stand a soldier before a high barrier - he will fret, becoming unnerved and weary, wondering what world awaits beyond the barrier. Thus, he will turnabout, returning to the humdrum world that pains him most. In the morrow, the soldier will wake again, just to cower once more.

If so guts are the measure of a soldier's strength, then it is so that a soldier is most feeble. He finds zeal in the ally, the breezeway, and the vestibule, forgoing the possibility of attaining residency at the Astoria. However, the *boss* is a boss. His footprint is boundless, spanning from New York to Havana to Italy. Thus, once you have opted for a life in *the life*, you ought to invest totally, knowing that you are *superior to most men.* Be it noble or ignoble, the path in which you choose ought to receive your uppermost effort. If you take *scores* hijacking cargo, your heist ought to be *Lufthansa;* if you are a labor racketeer, *Hoffa* and his *Teamsters* ought to be in your pocket.

Be it yesterday, nowadays, or the morrow, if you invest one-half, a mere one-half will be your *take.* Thus, you ought to stand two feet in *this thing of ours*, where you are *made.* Truth: If you so choose the *Cosa Nostra, our thing* ought to precede God, country, spouse, and next of kin. Just as a sportsman shoots at the hoop, a statesman votes on the bill, and a woman lays to be entered, if you forgo P.S 10 in exchange for *the life*, you ought to holster *pistolas* and frolic with the racketeers. All which you stand for must be of racket interest. If so the rackets bring you life, then so the rackets ought to bring you death.

Truth: To be a *man of honor*, you must be prepared to suffer immensely and perish in the company of whom you love, for such is the only pathway to *Boss.* Thus, once you have risen to the senior post, you ought to stand before your family and declare to the soldiers that in both life and death, you are God – the boss of the bosses, and all men stand far distant from your glory, and will so for a time unending.

Truth: A boss ought to lay for whatsoever he stands, and for whatsoever he lives, he ought to die for, too. Thus, if you live by the rule that *the boss is your boss*, you are to die by the rule that *the boss is your boss*.

Rule #7
<u>Be Vigilant of Your Rivals</u>

"We have to go to the mattress again. We have to get rid of these people." - **Salvatore Maranzano**

A boss ought not to be distracted by his racket success. Be it that the bootleg operation is booming and the city elites beg of your counsel, naught ought to cause you to become lax in your focus. As a lowly soldier, you were vigilant and skeptical. You moved with the wariness of a feline, distrusting of your public and the government therein. Thus, as boss, be it that *the Commission* yields to your every demand; be it that the millions arrive in lots of one score; be it that *Carmine DeSapio* and the governor's office beg of your dollars, you ought not to be so foolish as to subscribe to the notion that your family is bulletproof. Respectability, influence, and cash fraught coffers do not make you impregnable. Just as the bullet penetrates the soldier, the bullet penetrates the boss. Thus, in spite of the Time cover which you grace, the news clippings flush with your name, the booming construction racket, and too, the three federal indictments that the jurymen returned in your favor, you ought to know when your foe is near.

Glitz and glamour causes a soldier to suspend his guard. He – the soldier, will become lax at the tongue and blind to the world. Ruin will surely ensue. When fraught with success, the soldier will bebop at the discotheque and sniff of the powder which be for the *coloreds*. He will drink the *vino* in excess and bet the stallions to a negative. Truth: When fattened – Pockets bulging, the soldier is destructive. His success is of the moment and his death is imminent. The bullet will strike by way of his own silliness.

If ever you shine bright, your aura will be observed. A chauffeured Lincoln and three piece attire is of high cost. Further, quality loafers conceal a shine and three acquittals at the magistrate gives pause to your rivals. For your dapper appeal and the Lincoln which you ride, the newsman will write of you. You are picture perfect, and what is photo-friendly lures lights and lenses. For the three indictments that the adjudicators cleared, you will be typecast the *Teflon Don*. Thus, you will be crowned king – hailed as the messiah by your public and its newsmen. However, the messiah you are not. You are a boss, and even *Don Vito,* the most ruthless of them all, will submit oneself to God. Truth: A boss is begrudged for his wealth and power, ergo, no man will submit to a boss with sincerity, for wealth and power invite pause, and a boss owns the deed to both.

As boss, is it not so that you are sought after by the most striking of womenfolk? Is it not too, so, that your dollars are long, stretching to and fro safe deposits in Zurich? Thus, you ought to reject the flattery of your public and the media therein. In the morning when you wake and in the night when you slumber, you rise and fall to ten enemies that will relish in your doom. Once you have succeeded to the pinnacle of the family, your enemies will begin to hug you; every anecdote in which you utter will draw laughter, and every idea in which you proffer will be accepted absent of opposition. However, you ought not to be fooled, for there is an assassin in close vicinity, and his gun aims for your noodle. Truth: Your enemy stands before you at dusk; your enemy stands before you at dawn. He too, runs your errands in the evenings, speaking on your behalf.

Who is your enemy? Truth: Look to thy right and your enemy will appear – It is your underboss; it is your topmost friend. Truth: Your enemy is he whom sits closest to you. He is whom you trust most. Truth: When the hammer comes down, look not to the soldier as the culprit. The man behind the gun will be your underboss. Truth: Your second-in-command and most senior of adviser's – the underboss - it is he whom is your enemy. Truth: To be the boss is to die by the hands of betrayal.

Envelopes fraught with the *lira,* an abundance of women, and endorsements from ranking men, will cause a soldier to feel untouchable. However, a day has yet to mark where any one thing has remained constant. What lies before you today will alter in the morrow. Thus, you ought not to be fooled by the beauty within the moment. When the streets are mum and the coast is clear, your estate will soon be under siege. You are near death and your most ardent enemy is closing in on you.

Rule #8
Break the Rules

"The minute I get out, I'm killing this motherfucker." - **Frank Locascio**

In *the life*, the boss sends for his underlings, calling them to the carpet to convey the family rules. *If you break rules, you end up in a dumpster.* Unbeknownst to the soldiers, rules are written to protect the interest of the boss - nothing more. The boss will make claim that the rules are unwavering and harsh to insure the longevity of the family. Truth: Rules are drawn and enforced to safeguard the interest of authority: the boss, while disenfranchising the common: the soldier. Thus, you ought not to subscribe to the rhetoric of your boss, for even he - the topmost authority, is lax in honor and disinterested in matters that do not promote the family.

A soldier is to recuse himself from even extending a mere handshake to the boss. If gratitude is to be extended, it is at the behest of the boss. As a soldier, you are not permitted to accost your boss for gratification. Be it that the matter is grave and your caporegime is of nil support, your dissent is to be voiced through an intermediary – the *consigliere*. You will have no access to the boss. He will shy away in his *White House* estate, aloof to your needs and cold to your worries.

To make the family work for you, you will have to take over the reins and rewrite the rules. Your boss must die. For how long will you permit your boss to eat from your rackets? For how long will you kill men whom you harbor no ill sentiment toward? For how long will you *Ducks* the law, wasting away years in Dannemora, and be *called to the carpet* for violations which you did not commit? Truth: If so you are a two decade tenured soldier, then so, for two decades you will suffer under the aforementioned. Until you rewrite the rules, your pains will persist.

To rewrite the rules, you must disrupt the family order. As order diminishes, as will the boss's power. Truth: The road that leads to *Boss* bears high risk. Where risk is absent, there exist no reward. To rule the family, you must oppose the rules that you have sworn to obey. Oblige not, and never so shall you rise to the high mark of the family. Truth: A boss will eliminate anyone that poses a threat to his family. If found in violation of a rule, the boss will quickly execute you. He will do so without hesitation, guilt, or fear of retribution, for a soldiers rank is scanty and insignificant. You will be executed and dismembered without the passing of a second thought.

To lead the family, there exist but one pathway: You must break the rules set forth by your boss, and you must do so undetected. As you break the rules – distributing narcotics and killing *made* men, be sure to never challenge the boss. Oblige not, and your expulsion will come quick. Be it so that you have killed *Little Nicky Scibetta* - your brother-in-law, called *the Chin* to execute your partner, and fingered *Paul* and *Jimmy the Gent* in the *Lufthansa case*, you ought to be spit-shine clean in the eyes of your boss.

If you are unwilling to break rules, your seating will be reserved at a table of soldiers. To rule the family you must first advance in rank, for it is of rarity that a soldier will speak to the boss. Bosses talk to bosses, not soldiers. Thus, you must rise in rank until you are called to *the Commission meets*. It is in the *meets* where you are close enough to converse with the bosses. Thus, as a soldier, you must rise from soldier to caporegime, from caporegime to underboss. You ought not to submit to rules. Rules are drawn to maintain order, and above all, a boss finds glee in order, as in the absence of order, soldiers are self-governed. When order is absent, all that which is strong will be weakened; what is advanced will be normalized, and what is abundant will grow scarce. However, you are not in a position to cause disorder from a mere soldiers rank. You must rise into the family's leadership. To effect change, at the bottommost, you must rise to caporegime, for a soldier's cry will not make way to the boss's ear.

Once you have risen into the hierarchy of the family, you are close enough to strike your boss. Kill him. Take over the family and rewrite the rules – Rules even more stringent than that of your predecessor. You must now protect yourself, for a new young soldier is rising within your family. He aspires to be the boss, and so he will be.

Rule #9
<u>Dress with a Dapper Appeal</u>

"I had on a beautiful double-breasted dark oxford gray suit, a plain white shirt, a dark blue silk tie with little tiny horseshoes on it. I had a charcoal gray herringbone cashmere topcoat with a Cavanagh gray fedora." – Lucky Luciano

The most polished among the soldiers adopt a boss's way-of-dress. A boss whom appears dashing and to the nines, will conduct oneself with heightened levels of sophistication and will exert a confidence and charm unbeknownst to that of casual appeal. A boss clothes oneself with formality, knowing that at a moment's notice, he may be summoned to an ad hoc *meet* with the heads of the *five families*. Truth: Even when accompanied by the slothful, the dapper man is not looked upon with disgust, but rather envy.

A soldier is ill-prepared, working his rackets in denim, whereas a boss has a barber and stylist *come every single day* to *shampoo his hair* - To *cut it, blow-dry it, comb and shape it*. The barber *finds the little things. He snips this and that – snips the hair in* the nostrils and inner ear. The boss is the boss. He presents himself as the *capo di tutti capi*, appearing dashing in high value attire, cut in pieces of three and tailored by Brioni. He has *a couple dozen suits, sports jackets, all kinds of shirts and turtle necks, ties, shoes all shined up, socks,* and *a hankie for his coat pocket.* His automobile – It is a Mercedes Benz. It is *washed and cleaned* every day. *Not even a speck can be on or in the car.* Thus, in all times, you ought to present oneself cleanly, with unmatched apparel, and the boss will view you as a man worthy of promotion. Appear whiskered and sullied, and you will forever work among the lowly – in the brothels and *carpet joints*.

No matter the affair, you ought to be of sharp dress. Be it so that the *meet* is held in a back alley, where it reeks of urine and feces, and the attendees are madams and pimps, you ought to stand in the midst of such foulness as if it were the *Atlantic City Conference*. Naught ought to forgo your appearance. Oblige not, and for a time of always, you will be looked upon as a mere *friend of mine*, rather a *friend of ours*. Truth: Appear as a soldier and so a soldier you will be.

Rule #10
<u>Kill the Boss</u>

"When you become boss in this life, you don't get elected. You eliminate the boss above you." - **Michael Franzese**

Truth: Naught is sacred; all is unholy.

If ever you are at odds with your boss, in your absence, he plots against you, and in a time not long, you will be no more. Once the boss has marked you as a truant, there exists no reversal for his sentiment. Death will find you. Thus, you must take arms and rise against him. You ought not to cower. Truth: A soldier dies on his knees; a boss dies on his *mattress*.

Your boss is not an enemy that is easy to kill. When you rise, you ought to be dressed in a manner that is suitable for death, for if your attempt is botched, you will be killed before the barrel of your revolver spins but once. The boss will kill you – harshly. Your death will be painful and you will be used as an example. You will have your hands chopped off, your tongue will be cut from your mouth; your throat will be slit; your penis will be severed and left in your throat, and after you have suffered immensely, your limbs and head will be removed and stuffed into a cement barrel and dropped into the East River. You will not be given a proper burial; your remains will never be recovered, and your next of kin will mourn for a lifetime, pondering your whereabouts, unsure as to whether you are dead or alive.

Truth: Your boss is *a fish on the desert. He* is *a fish out of water. He don't know this life.* He is *a rat, yellow dog* – a *pansy* and a *milk drinker.* He is long tenured, and a long tenured boss is most arrogant. His decades of unopposed headship have blurred his vision. He has grown fat and slothful, drinking *vino* and eating of the pasta. He is aloof to the streets. He is not a *gangster*, he is *a racketeer.* He meets with *the Commission;* he reads the Wall Street Journal; his dialog is with the bosses. He has grown complacent and out of touch, and for such, he must go.

As you rise within the family ranks, being promoted from *associate* to soldier, soldier to caporegime, and caporegime to underboss, your growth will be stymied once you reach the second most senior rank – Underboss. Your final promotion – from underboss to boss must come by way of self. Your boss whom has guided and blanketed you north of a decade, *made* you, and made you rich, teaching you the rackets and promoting you within his family, must now die. Oblige not, and a boss's rank will forever elude you.

Truth: *All that Costello* knew, he *stole.* Is it not so that you have stolen your boss's ambition for the rackets and his legislative contacts? Is it not so that you have adopted his cunning in acquiring new rackets and eliminating rival factions? Is it not too, so, that you have stolen his cold persona and his lax regard for honor and loyalty? Truth: You have worked the streets at the behest of the boss; you have committed murder in counts by the dozen. Your nights on the *mattress* and the scar that disfigures your face, all have arisen by way of the boss and your affection for his family. Thus, every bullet that you pump into your boss is warranted. He has earned every shot. Blood ought to spat from his face; knives ought to enter his chest, and the sharpest blade ought to slice his throat fully, from left to right, ear to ear. Truth: As your boss gasp for one last breath and then lay dead before you, if your tailored fabrics are not sodden with blood then you missed a spot. To *keep on living and keep on moving up,* your boss must die. Truth: A boss will not surrender his family. His power must be usurped. Truth: A boss ought not to be left to live. Oblige not and he will avenge you later.

Once you have risen in wealth and influence, your boss will become weary of you – fearful that you are becoming too powerful. Thus, you must submit to your boss fully, proving your willingness to be subservient even though your pockets are fat and your influence extends long. Truth: Before rising to boss, your boss too, was first an underboss. Hence, he knows how you think. He knows that you vie to rule the family. Thus, you will be pulsed as to whether or not you are a threat. If found to be a threat, the boss will move on you – organizing your ousting by way of the bullet. However, an underboss is not easily ousted, for his power is long, making him more difficult to unseat.

A boss will not move against an underboss with the same expedients as he would if weary of a soldier. An underboss is influential and highly regarded by the soldiers. By the time one has risen to underboss, respectability among the caporegimes, the *consigliere*, and the soldiers, has been garnered. An underboss has contacts in the legislator and the commissioner's office. Thus, if ever the boss rises against his underboss without cause, the family will split in two. One half the caporegimes will align with the boss; one half the caporegimes will align with the underboss. The family will be at war until one side is eliminated and a new boss is inducted by *the Commission*. Truth: Wartime's bring about disorder. When order is lax, a boss is vulnerable.

As an underboss grows in strength, the boss has two options: Align with his underboss or kill him. If the underboss is viewed as a truant, the boss will favor the latter and forgo the former. However, if the underboss continues to work the union locals, attend *meets* without ruckus, and turn in $2 million before the close of twelve months, the boss will spare the life of his underboss, viewing him as trustworthy. Truth: If ever you have been marked as a truant and yet your boss attempts to align with you, he is buying time. In your absence, he plots against you, drawing plans to weaken you; stealing your resources and ordering hits against your top loyalist. Once your power has waned and your loyalist *sleep with the fishes*, your boss will eliminate you.

You ought not to trust a boss. The boss is fraught with wealth and power. Thus, he lives by a questionable creed. For a boss, more important than shiny things and next of progeny, is the family and the power exercised therein. Thus, if ever you are at odds with the boss, your options are limited. You must act swiftly and kill him or he will beat you to it. When threatened, the boss will not hold a *sit-down*, nor will he hear your justification. He will course no action or alternate plan that deviates from putting a hole in your head. Thus, if ever given the chance to usurp the boss, with expedience and without dialog or timidity, you ought to fire a deadly round into his skull.

In all times, be it noble or ignoble, you ought not to surrender until the boss is dead and you are at the helm of the family. Truth: To rule the family, your boss must die. If unwilling to kill the boss, you are not fitted for headship, for every boss, both long tenured and the contrary, has first parked their life at the entrance of death, before rising to *Boss*. Truth: The price of *Boss* is your life. Thus, if unwilling to pay with your life, you will forever occupy a soldier's rank. Senior to all, what separates the boss from his soldier counterpart is fearlessness. Be it the threat of the chair, *on the lamb* - hiding out from a team of assassin's, or 50 years in Dannemora, a boss is fearless and works with impunity.

To be a boss, you will have to fight a boss at every level. The same boss that you once served with honor and efficiency, will be the very boss that you have to snipe. If you are an *Associate*, your boss - the *Soldier,* whom mentored and guided you, must die for you to assume his post. If you are a *Soldier*, your boss - the *Caporegime*, whom mentored and guided you, must die for you to assume his post. If you are a *Caporegime*, your boss - the *Underboss*, whom mentored and guided you, must die for you to assume his post. If you are an *Underboss*, your boss - the *Boss*, whom mentored and guided you, must die for you to assume his post and take the reins of the family. You ought not to leave the family on a bent knee. *Go to the mattresses,* and *if it means you have to die there, then die there. Die there in a gun battle with the cops* – but *do not back off of* the *hit.* If you must die, stand there and die; die with guns drawn, as it is better to die standing up than to live sitting down.

Truth: When you kill your boss, do so with honor: Shoot him in the face with his eyes open.

Rule #11
Accept Risk

"If I get 50 years, I know what I got to do." – **John Gotti**

The bosses of *the Commission* have been awarded in abundance. Their wealth will spend for a day past forever; their influence resides in every high office in New York State, and their respectability met hands with Hoover, Roosevelt, Mussolini, and Batista. All which a boss has attained: the plushest of real property, fawning escorts, and cash fraught Zurich accounts - all have come by way of risk and sacrifice.

When risk yields its face, the soldier begins to fret. Try as you may, a small risk will not yield a generous reward. Safe, low risk rackets yield safe, low risk returns. Thus, to be the boss, you ought to fill a box with your most cherished valuables, and hedge it on a long shot. Only then will you reap tenfold the box.

Safe hedging – a soldiers gamble, turns nominal gains, but the boss will wager the entire box, every time, every bet, without fear of regression, humiliation, or starting anew. You ought not to be bamboozled into believing that your rise will come absent of scrutiny or impedance. Truth: A day will arise where you are called to undertake a monumental task, and unwaveringly, you ought to oblige and succeed. You ought not to fail. To fail will expel you from promotion, and never so shall you *father* the family.

Before you are *made* and welcomed into the family, you will be tested. Your test will come by way of the boss. He will *send for you, calling you to the carpet,* ordering you *to go on a piece of work the following day.* Truth: The boss will need you to kill an adversary. You will be ordered to assemble a hit squad and carry out the *job* with excellence, leaving no witnesses or trail of evidence. You ought not to fail, for in a man's times, he is granted one opportunity to be *made* and inducted into a society of secrecy. Thus, no matter the request, you ought to accept whatsoever the boss asks of you. Be it that the boss directs you to walk a mile high, one thousand foot long, tight rope – you must cross it, and you ought not to fail. Truth: For every ten attempts, nine men will plunge to their death; one will prevail, for being the boss is not for the faint at heart. Truth: Your destiny awaits at the end of the rope. Your boss, the boss of your boss, and the bosses of past times, have crossed the mile high, one thousand foot, tight rope, and for such, the boss is your boss. You ought to follow suit. Oblige not, and a soldier's rank will forever be your zenith.

There is *only one head of the brotherhood in America,* and your chance at the throne arrives but once in a lifetime. Thus, if it is the *brotherhood* which you seek, be it that the barrel of a shotgun rest at your skull, you ought to take your chance, and go for the throne. Oblige not, and the remainder of your life will be spent in agony. Truth: *Be it an hour from now, or be it tonight, or a hundred years from now,* you ought not to pass on your chance to lead the family. From the morning of your inception until the night of your abortion, you ought to seize every opportunity that leads to a boss's rank.

Truth: If the choices are to be a soldier or die, far better to die than to live like a soldier.

Rule #12
<u>Align with the High Rank</u>

"It takes many steppingstones for a man to rise. None can do it unaided." **– Joseph Bonanno**

Courting the favor of a soldier is futile. If you are a racketeer, running rum from the maritime limit to the Harlem speakeasies, you ought to court not the favor of the officer, but rather the favor of the commissioner, as if even the captain vies for your arrest, you have the protection of the higher authority – the commissioner. By controlling the commissioner, you exert influence over the entire precinct.

For you are the boss, you ought to align with the influential, the powerful, and every man of high rank. Oblige so, and you will inherit all which falls beneath them. If a union president can be bought, buy him, and you will adopt his locals. If a police commissioner can be bribed, pay him what is due, and you will adopt his captain. By aligning with the captain, you will inherit the officers, giving you command over the streets in which they patrol. If in need of the city, court the favor of the mayor. By aligning with the mayor, you will inherit the councilmen and the laborers. If in need of political muscle, court the favor of the delegates, for even a Kennedy is unelectable when absent of the delegates.

To lead a family, you are needing of influence, dollars, and public respectability. All acts in which you undertake ought to be harmonious and bring rise to the aforesaid. Be it that you are aligned with soldiers amounting to one thousand, what power can you exercise if the caporegimes push for your ouster? Is it not so that the soldiers work at the behest of the caporegime? Further, if you are aligned with caporegimes amounting to two dozen, what power can you wield if the underboss pushes for your ouster? Is it not so that the caporegimes work at the behest of the underboss? Thus, to exert influence, you ought to have control of the highest authority. Be it that the boss gives orders to the underboss, you ought to align with the boss, supplying him a valued service and an *envelope* at the turn of each month. Oblige so, and you will inherit the underboss, the caporegimes, and the soldiers.

A soldier works the streets absent of a gun. He is a fool - he will stand in a construction site absent of a cement pale and hardhat. All is to lose and naught is to gain when accompanied by the soldier. Henceforth, be it thy next of kin, if ever a man carries the face of a soldier, you ought to move far from his company. Chop him off just as you would the hands of *Sonny Black*. To invite a soldier into the uppermost echelon of the family is to spur your own decadence. Your underboss and caporegimes ought to be late seasoned and gray. They are your advisers and they oversee your *white*, high dollar rackets.

Ranking men ought to be your advisors, your friends, and they ought to be on your payroll. If a senator has power, align with him. Make him your friend. If a banker and newspaperman wield influence, you ought to befriend them, too. The power that you exercise outside of the family will fortify the power that you exercise within. The police commissioner and the governor's office ought to be your friend. You will need said relationships during time of trial.

Truth: The family is fraught with racketeers and gangsters. Thus, be it your most polished of men, a jury will not warm to the testimony of a gangster, for *a gangster is a guy who is real tough. He's a street guy; he's a street hoodlum.* However, the commissioner is the law and the governor is a statesman. Such men will sway a jury and a weary public, and their legitimacy will pose for good public relations when you need it most.

Rule #13
<u>Speak Nothing – Mums the Word</u>

**"*Don't ever say anything you don't want played back to you someday.*" -
John Gotti**

Upon introduction – be it *a friend of mine* or *a friend of ours*, a soldier will be loose at the tongue, disclosing his *take* in the *numbers* and critical facets of his function. He will detail the name of his spouse, the location of his kin, his disdains and annoyances, and where he holds court. As boss, you ought not to interrupt a soldier spewing from the mouth. Let him speak, for as sure as the Italians kill their own, a day will arise where the talkative soldier must be *clipped*. His parrot way-of-speak will write the plans for his own execution. Truth: Chattiness invites the law with its indictment tagging alongside, bringing about the decimation of all *five families*.

Truth: *Ferrara's* has the *best cannoli*. Thus, if it is said that your rival dines on Italian pastries six-and-one-half hours post dusk, the stink of the corpse must come a half past noon, and the carcass must lay at the door of *Ferrara's*. Is not the soldier of loose lips? Truth: A soldier dies by the gun, the knife, and too, his words.

The hitman frets not his order to *whack* a soldier, for *whacking* a soldier requires no skill, whereas a steady hand is required when moving on a boss. As the boss speaks naught in the presence of his men and leads the *borgata* with few words, how ought one to conspire against him? Truth: If so a man be lax with his tongue, his edifice will be most difficult to breach.

Much talking brings about *Giuliani* and his agents, whereas silence brings a man no worries. Where the soldier is freely expressive, the boss is reserved and absent of speech, knowing that wheresoever words are present, as is the ear of *Giuliani*. Thus, the boss is a *Don* and the soldier is a *stool pigeon*. Truth: In all matters, you ought to speak without inclusion of the tongue. When a boss nods, the soldiers go to war – *mattresses* move from tenement to tenement, arms turn to limbs, and lime buries the stench of the carcass.

Truth: When the boss orders a hit, he does so by way of gesture. He nods his head; he taps his *Chin*. He speaks with his eyes, his hands, yet never his mouth. Truth: What is born in the mouth will die in the ear. Thus, you ought not to speak incriminating words or share in dialog that warrants the bullet. If you must speak, you ought to speak to the maître d', the plantsman, and the maiden. When addressing the family, speak only what does not bring about indictment. You are the boss - as you wake, you wake to a world of envy, where the caporegimes and the soldiers await your dismay. The law and rival factions eavesdrop on your *walk-talks* and your daughters *pink phone* is being wiretapped. Further, the *Ravenite* is bugged, as is your chauffeured Jaguar and the dwelling on the second floor. Truth: Naught is a secret once it has left the topmost of your neck.

In your yawns – both dusk and dawn, there waits a mole at your front and back. Smoke and mirrors are the face of the family. Thus, be vigilant with whom you speak. You ought not to be bamboozled. Every smile is a frown in disguise. There exist not a friend in the company of a boss. Truth: Where wealth and power hold court, at what table is there seating for a friend? A friend is made to give credence to an enemy; trust is granted to give credence to betrayal. In all times, you ought not to trust a man whom speaks with a familiar tongue; walks upright, and holds ten toes, eight fingers, and two thumbs. Such a man will be careless with your words. Thus, you ought to be lax in all of your speech. Oblige so, and on the day of your trial, there will not exist a man whom can turn state's evidence and bring about your demise.

The soldier permits the tongue to flap freely, without pause or regard for law enforcement or wiretaps. Truth: While your rackets are illicit and 19 carcasses wear your bullet, such crimes will not bring about your ruin. As sure as the *French* have a *connection*, your downfall will come by way of the tongue. You will unknowingly formulate the plot that puts a bullet in your cranium. When the lawman raids your social club, indicting you, your underboss, and your *consigliere*, the smoking gun will be a recording device, bearing the sound of your voice. Thus, you ought to guard your tongue as you would the conspiracy of the family. Oblige so, and prolonged rule will be the result.

While the soldier rambles, detailing hit-jobs and the asbestos and concrete rackets, the boss speaks with the lips of a dead man. For the kiss denotes death and has *killed a lot of guys*, if you speak in a non-verbal manner, you can kill all of your enemies and guilt will be most difficult to prove.

The soldier is an open book. He speaks absent of a filter and incriminates himself and his partners. As boss, you ought to speak naught; mums the word, for the ear of your enemy is close by. While you assumed the walls as deaf, there was a bug concealed in the crevices beneath your stool. The jury will hear the audio playback in federal court. Your *Gambino* family and all which you have gained will be no more. You will spend your final hours in Marion Correctional, pleading with your daughter to send *a group picture of* your *grandchildren*. Your properties will be seized, your son will be indicted, your grandson will aspire to be a crook, and you are *going to die before* your daughter has *a toothache.*

Rule #14
<u>Impose Harsh Rules</u>

"We don't break our captains. We kill them." – **Vincent "the Chin" Gigante**

The boss calls a *meet*, summoning his soldiers amounting to five scores. Standing before the family, the boss states that the sun relaxes at dusk, at which time each soldier has until the cool of the morning to collect and return ten troughs of whiskey. Making no exception, the boss notes that be it all one hundred or one, any soldier whom falls short of his directive will lose his life. Continuing, the boss states that be it all one hundred or one, any soldier whom meets his directive will keep his life and be awarded a fifth of Scotch and a *puttana* of good lay.

Awoken by the morning cool, the boss accost his soldiers. Four scores and 19 are less ten troughs. One soldier has met his directive, presenting ten troughs of whiskey to the boss. Without dialog or counsel, the boss ought to call his under-performing soldiers to the carpet, severing their heads, one-by-one. Following the thud of 99 heads hitting the floor, the accomplished soldier ought to be awarded said *puttana* and fifth of Scotch. His diligence ought to be noted, yet not in excess, for more will be required of him.

Holding court at the *Ravenite*, the boss is unable to make contact with his *capodecina*. The boss fumes: *"I called your fucking house five times yesterday! Now, if you're going to disregard my motherfucking phone calls, I'll blow you and that fucking house up! If I ever hear anybody else calls you and you respond within five days, I'll fucking kill you!"*

The night turns and the morning comes. The boss rises and phones his *decina*, to no avail. Five days suspend and yet mums the word. As promised, you – the boss, ought to send for your top gunner, directing him to assemble a team of assassin's, igniting the home of your insubordinate *capodecina*. At the top of the morning, the headlines ought to read: MASSIVE EXPLOSION LEAVES HOME IN RUBBLE – ONE DEAD.

A soldier is most difficult to manage. His rank is lowly, he is absent of independence, and his rackets turn nickels. Thus, be it in line with the rules or outside thereof, if a dollar is to be gained, it will be sought by the soldier. However, as boss, you ought not to be tolerant of defiance. In the most laconic of speak, you ought to make clear to your family that cement feet await any member found in violation of the rules. Be it one or one hundred, all violators ought to feel the warmth of a bullet penetrate their skull. Truth: Disobedience is to be dealt with by way of the gun.

Is it not so that the boss stood before the family and declared that *no man must ever, upon penalty of death, talk about the organization or the family of which he* is *a member, not even within his own home*? Is it not so that the boss noted *every man must obey, without question, the orders of the leader above him*, and that *no man must ever strike another member, regardless of the provocation*? Is it not so that while holding the podium, standing at the helm of the *meet*, the boss declared that *all grievances to this day, imagined or real*, are *to be forgiven and total amnesty granted*? Is it not so that the boss made clear that *no man* can *ever covet another's business or another's wife*, and *if you do, you pay with your life*? Thus, as you - the boss, were clear in your orders, you ought not to spare the life of an insubordinate soldier. Oblige not, and your soldiers will run amuck, viewing your orders as weak – on shaky legs and lacking significance.

A soldier learns not by rhetoric, but rather by way of the bullet and or the burial of cherished kin. The mere threat of a bullet will not deter a soldier. However, the warmth of a bullet teaches a soldier much. Next of kin must perish and legs must become limp. How ought a man to utter when absent of a tongue? Thus, if ever a man speak too loosely, remove his tongue, and never more will his rhetoric be of concern. When dealing with your soldiers, you ought to be direct in all of your speech: *Do you want to wake up in the morning, don't see your son no more? Is that what you desire?*

As boss, you will locate defiance under every leaf in the family. Thus, if ever you are to levy a threat, it ought to be levied with true intent. Your family ought to know that when you speak, your words are true. Your penalties ought to be enforced harshly and swiftly. Stand your loyalist in the presence of the defiant, and execute every defiant man, point blank range, one-by-one. Remove their tongue with which they speak and their hand with which they shake. Stack their limbs in a pile, and let the stench of death breathe into the air, bringing nausea to your loyalist. Oblige so, and a defiant soldier will be your worry no more.

Rule #15
<u>Avoid Routine</u>

"I don't create a pattern in my life. I don't walk my dog 7 o'clock in the morning, every morning. I don't go to the same restaurant, sit in the same seat every Tuesday night." – **Michael Franzese**

A boss ought to shy away from routine. If a *meet* is scheduled at the *Bergin Hunt*, and on every week's fifth day, you call your soldiers to appear, reporting on their *take*, sooner before later, you will be infiltrated. The law watches you from due-East and *Chin* knows of your location. Thus, you ought not to call your soldiers on a fixed schedule. Oblige not, and as sure as the *coloreds* bet *000*, you will fall by the hands of a rival.

Be it that the family met on week four, day six of the first month, the succeeding *meet* ought to have no correlation. Hence, it ought to be scheduled on week two, day three, two months following the first. Oblige so, and your rivals will be scrambled. Truth: A boss is most easily penetrated when boxed in a four wall enclosure. Be it an automobile, an office, an eatery, or a social club, if routine is a must, do so in a setting absent of four walls.

In all that you do, naught ought to be of routine. If you regularly break bread and toast grapes with an in-law, the time, day, and location of which you meet ought to differ. If it is known that you sniff a rose bush on the twelfth hour of every third week's fourth day, it is of certainty that your last day will come in the presence of a rose bush.

You ought not to be so foolish as to enter into matrimony with any one idea or strategy, for even perfection conceals a hairline crack. Thus, try as you may - fence your estate with twelve foot barriers, topped with barbed wire; permit the dogs to bark loudly and armed men to roam the terrain; have the estate swept for bugs and every crevice under surveillance – if ever you hold court in a routine location, your end will come the day before the morrow.

Rule #16
Keep a Stash – Money Speaks Every Language

"I got plenty of dough." – Lucky Luciano

Truth: The dollar purchases an answer to all things. As head of the family, a large cache of monies ought to be on reserve in Zurich, held for the morning where the lawmen ransack your quarters. Truth: Five to one your *take* ought to be on reserve. Thus, if your racket turns one million, your hideaway ought to count five-fold. Truth: The Lincoln rides as smooth as butter and the *signet* ring projects a shine, but above diamonds and gold, luxury automobiles and plush residency, a boss ought to have monies that pile high. It will be at your dimmest hour – on a day where you are least prepared, that the law lights flash and the family erupts into uprising. It will be your Zurich reserves that buy you time.

When sirens blare and the state brings indictment, your legal expense will be $700,000 and your bail will be high, set at $350,000. Further, when your rival kidnaps your closest of kin, the ransom note will read with six zeros. And just when you thought that the sun would always shine, the IRS will raid your headquarters, handing you a debt receipt, humiliating you publicly. In the end, your most profitable racket will bottom out, reducing your revenue one half. Truth: If your cup is dry, you are useless to none. Thus, your stash box ought to go deep enough to blanket you during time of scrutiny. You ought to be able to make payment to your creditors and partners.

A boss ought not to go penniless in the eyes of his public. He ought to be cash rich. The public ought to view a boss as a man of high wealth. Truth: The poor man is a shame. He brings shame to self and his kinfolk look upon him with disgust.

If you are not in a position to buy or trade, then you are a *crumb, working and slaving for a few bucks.* Your world moves you, rather than you moving your world. Your shame ought to bring about the most grime and agonizing of labor, cleansing the commode and the feces and foulness therein. Your boss ought to work you until your *hands* are *roughen*ed and fraught with *calluses.*

The coffers of a boss overflow with cash, valuables, and all which holds glimmer and shine. Thus, as boss, you ought to pile your dollars to an innumerable sum and collect valuables until none are left remaining. Every mattress, shoe-box, hole-in-the-wall, car trunk, and duffle-bag, ought to be fraught with cash. As sure as *Lucchese* is absent a forefinger and thumb, a day will present itself where payola is required. Ergo, you will need to draw from your stash and make payment where payment is due.

Bribery and corruption are creatures that are close confidants of the boss, and said creatures eat envelopes of green dollars. Every deed has a price; every favor conceals a motive. Naught is done for sheer love. Thus, your emotions are to be checked and reserved for thy family, whereas reason and brute are to be reserved for the *family*, as when absent of emotion, the cash cache folds bigly.

Rule #17
Loyalty is a Canard – Show None, Expect None

"When I looked around the neighborhood, I found out that the kids wasn't the only crooks. We was surrounded by crooks, and plenty of them was guys who were supposed to be legit, like the landlords and storekeepers and the politicians and cops on the beat. All of them was stealing from somebody." **- Lucky Luciano**

A soldier falls for hocus-pocus with ease. His price is fairly cheap. He will barter his loyalty for a small *policy* racket and offer you friendship, unknowing that such is a fable. Truth: If ever a better opportunity arises, a soldier will kill his boss in a jiffy.

The dollar is a soldier's king. If a coin is to be gained, a soldier will sell his loyalty for cheap. Be it an *outsider*, boss or underboss, caporegime or soldier, when has time marked where a man's honor has not been offered for sale? Truth: If it is so that man has strode the planet for 1,000 years, then it is too, so, that for 1,000 years a man's honor could be purchased at low cost.

If there exist but one link that tethers a boss and a soldier, it is their lax regard for loyalty. While the price may differ, there exists not a soldier nor a boss whom will not betray their partners. Truth: Betrayal causes a soldier to fret, whereas a boss relishes in the moment, knowing that betrayal is the price of headship.

As boss, are you so foolish that you expect to be in holding of all of the wealth, all of the power, and all of the respect, while never being betrayed by your soldiers? If so, you are a fool and a fool falls to folly. As the head of the family, you ought to anticipate betrayal. If you have yet to be betrayed, then you are in possession of naught which holds value, as what is valuable is sought after. Truth: A boss is under constant duress. He is persecuted, victimized, and lambasted by his public. His left hand will be made limp by his right hand counterpart. Thus, if you are not thick at the skin – brute enough to be riddled by the force of the Tommy gun, then you ought not to go for *Boss*.

A soldier's rank is absent of ridicule, public scrutiny, and infidelity among friends. Thus, if you aspire to be the boss, you ought to anticipate the *stool pigeons* to *sing*, the *Don Vitone's* to call *Chin*, the *Estes Kefauver's* to hold hearings, and the *Thomas Dewey's* to bring indictment. Truth: For whom you hold affection will soon be for whom you hold disdain. You will too, require protection from who was once your protector. Truth: If so a man has been riddled with ammunition, it is too, so, that before he was struck, he stared down the barrel of a revolver, as his best in friendship stood behind the sights, with his finger on the trigger.

Truth: If ever you are dumb to who is scheming and conspiring in the deafness of your ear and the blindness of your view, look not far beyond the topmost echelon of your family, and you will spot the culprit.

Once you have succeeded to the helm of the family, and the *borgata* and all therein is under your rule, you ought to be watchful of every eye. You are the boss - You are respected by the aristocrats and the commoners. You harbor long dollars and your name rings bells in the high offices of New York State. Thus, in the deaf of your ear, your soldier's muck up your standing. They utter harsh invectives: "*All he is interested in is making money."* Your underboss will join the fury: *"He's a stupid pig."* Thus, you ought to extend trust to no one. All who bow and kiss your *signet* do so in spite. If trust is to be granted, it ought to be granted to an enemy and naught thereafter, for of all whom are *made*, an enemy is the only man fitted for trust.

If ever your enemy decrees to kill you, he will make good on that which he has promised. Truth: Contempt moves a man more rapidly than affection. Thus, if ever you are marked on a man's *kill list,* trust that he will conspire until your name is no more.

Why doth a man fret? Why doth a man have a wide-eyed night and a sluggish day? Truth: Betrayal causes a man to mope. Be it a soldier who you *made* or a friend who was best, when the *sawed-off* turns your head into mush, the trigger man will be *Vito* – your friend. As you *smile and wave* your *hand*, warmly receiving *Vito*, he will blow your *head off*.

Truth: The tears that drip from the points of your lash and the brass that pierces that most vulnerable of your flesh, will be induced by a friend. Thus, you ought to omit all traces of trust from your being. If an exception is to be made, it ought to be made for an enemy.

A soldier is weak and trusting of all, hence the reason he works for you. Is it not so that only the weakest among men take orders? A boss *knows he is superior to most men*, thus, he opts not to be permitted, but rather to grant permission. Truth: A soldier subscribes to the ideals of loyalty. You ought not to follow him into the grave. Let him die. He lives a morbid life, sad – unsure as to why he is regularly betrayed. While he frets the bullet, he is unknowing that his heartbeat will cease by the foolishness of his trust. As sure as sunrise is the morning and sunset is the evening, and the moon gives face in the night, a man will always be lax in honor. A great many of great men were knifed in the back, and perished, choking on their own blood, and the culprit was a trusted confidant, who was *made*, and was of the same *Cosa Nostra*.

You are to look not far to locate an enemy. He is not well insulated. Look to thy right - whom dwells there? Truth: When the soil is ripe, it will be your right hand – your top loyalist, who riddles you with brass, spinning you backwards, leaving you face down in the drippings of your blood. As the vultures eat of your carcass, said loyalist will lay your spouse and paddle your progeny.

Rule #18
Pay Your Soldiers Well

"It's remarkable how loyal people will be when you look after them as well as we did. We gave them incentives and rewards for good work. When they came up with useful proposals, we praised them and lined their pockets." – Meyer Lansky

When monies are sparse and the rackets turn a loss, the honorable become thieves; priests become pimps, and the brute become cowards. The most honorable among men will suspend their loyalty if ever their efforts do not produce good pay. What soldier works among the muck, *with them niggers breathing down* their *neck*, without reason? Truth: A soldier frats with the lowly ranked because *junk* and *numbers* yield a good *take*. He too, works the *speaks* with the drunkards and the brothels with the *whores,* all in anticipation of being a *good earner*. Thus, if ever you look upon your soldier, and his blazer is sodden with blood and his trousers wear a knee hole, note that his work day was hard, and his efforts ought to come with good pay.

As boss, you ought to pay your soldier whatsoever is his due - in return, he will work his rackets with excellence. He will bestow upon you his loyalty. Truth: A boss must pay his soldiers a wage topping that of his rivals, for if the soldiers can be easily bought, the family will fall. Truth: It is better to kill a man than to misuse a man. Misuse a soldier and he will misuse you. Before pay – be it high or low, a man is needing of respectability. Thus, if ever a soldier is paid two dollars for a job valued at four, it will bring him pause. He will rise against you, sell your secrets, and bring the lawman to your door. To pay a man his due is a show of respect. Thus, as boss, you ought not to cheapen your soldier's honor by way of low compensation. Oblige so, and your soldier will *want to assure you of* his *loyalty,* proving that *it is unwavering.*

To prevent your family from falling into a *Banana War*, you ought to pay your soldiers three times what the market will bear. Bestow upon them the finest of Scotch, aged *vino*, penne pasta, mozzarella and tomato, pesto linguine, a flaky crust cannoli, and the freshest brewed Italian latte. A boss ought not to be fat while the family is malnourished. Why ought the soldiers to fret over the *lira* if so their price is cheap? Truth: If so the boss is fat, then so the soldiers ought to be fat.

A soldier is complacent. His loyalty can be bought for a low price. You ought to meet his asking, for it will be cheap, and will have nil effect on the family holdings. Truth: Pay a soldier his due, which will be nominal, and he will work his rackets with distinction, never seeking promotion or opting to resign from his post.

Rule #19
<u>Speak the Language of a Soldier</u>

"He tailored his speeches to the mentality of his audience. To a simple audience, he spoke in parables; to a more intelligent audience, he proclaimed ideas." – **Joseph Bonanno**

Truth: If the saints are to enter a hellish kingdom, operating under the governance of pious law, the hell-raisers will have their way, hence the saints will burn in a bath of fire. Thus, to live among the fools, a foolish tongue you ought to murmur; a foolish gait you ought to mimic; a foolish rationale you ought to harbor. Truth: If the soldiers are blind, the vision of the boss matters not.

As boss, you ought to speak to the family with a recognized dialect. The soldier is a hood. In the streets, he lives by the rules of the hard knocks. He is a gangster. He goes for the monies that pack high the big bag. Thus, if ever a soldier detects a profitable racket, be it peddling narcotics or working the *whores*, if the family approves in the amount of one half, you – the boss, ought not to stymie the soldier's initiative. You ought to leave him to his work. You ought to turn a blind eye.

Truth: You have declared to the family in whole that *anybody fucking around with junk, they got to be killed.* However, in your findings you discover that one half your soldiers and one half your rivals are *fucking around with junk.* What ought you – the boss – to do in response? Truth: It is not so that one half your family and one half your rivals are wrong. You ought not to take a gangster, dress him in tailored fabrics and chauffeur him in a Lincoln, and assume such a man to be white collar. If you *made* him as a gangster, then so a gangster he is. Thus, when you speak, you must speak as a gangster. Oblige not, and your words will fall on deaf ears. You will appear aloof in the eyes of your soldiers.

When you swing the pendulum, you ought to do so unhurriedly. Thus, if you attempt to legitimize the family - directing your soldiers to work *white rackets*, you ought to *make* new soldiers with white collar histories. You ought not to force a blue collar soldier to work white collar rackets. To do so is to invite pause among your soldiers, and uprising will ensue. Truth: The kennel affords food and shelter, yet the most abandoned and stray of hounds will resist, for that which is unknown is most unnerving. Thus, you ought to work a soldier in the rackets where he is most skilled. When you speak, speak to his work rather your own. Truth: You lead the soldiers and they sit before you in the *meet*. For such, you ought to speak with a tongue in which they identify. Speak to a soldier with the tongue of a banker and what will be heard is, "blah, blah."

A soldier would rather hate what he understands than to love what he does not. Thus, when leading the family, you ought to address your soldiers in a tongue that is familiar. Speak to their rackets, way-of-thought, and their persons. Truth: If a dollar is to be gained, it will be sought by the soldier. Be it narcotics – if in demand, you ought to let your soldier work. To invoke a ban on what is in high public demand will only invite decadence to your family. Truth: The soldier deals in narcotics because the profits are immense. Are the dollars of the *junk* less green than the *whores*? Is it not green dollars that the Madam turns in? Thus, you ought not to run a family fraught with illicit rackets and yet mandate your soldiers be legit. To do so is inept and your headship will appear foreign, bringing about a bullet which will meet your cranium.

A soldier thinks not with the mind of a boss. While the boss has a vision to see what is to come, a soldier is myopic, only seeing what is readily present. Thus, you - the boss, ought to utter naught in the presence of a soldier that he canst not comprehend. Oblige not, and you will be shot dead, alongside your chauffeur, and the soldier whom you baffled will assume your post.

Truth: A soldier mocks the vision of the blind and the comprehension of the deaf. Thus, in your headship, if ever you see beyond the mountains, where the soldier holds nil sight, mums the word. You ought to guide the soldier to his viewpoint: the mountain. When you reach the mountain, he will see your vision, and follow you further. If you speak your vision prior to reaching the mountain, your soldiers will mark you as weak and unwise – and they will kill you, fearful that your direction will bring down the family.

Rule #20
<u>Take It to the Mattress - When It's Time to Kill, Kill Everyone</u>

"If a man is in a fight, then he must fight to the end." – Joseph Bonanno

If ever a new direction must be sought, half will be with you; half will be against you. Neither side will be a benefactor to the family. If half oppose, more will follow. Thus, you ought to trust not the entire lot. Of all whom follow, one will be *Donnie Brasco*. Thus, if a new direction must be sought, it must come by means of war. All whom led the former regime must die. All enforcers and faction of the former regime must perish, too. Truth: *Whenever a boss dies, all his faithfuls have to go with him.* You ought to drop the hammer penetrating three levels south. Kill the sons and the sons of the sons if so they are *made* in *the life.* If life is to be spared, it ought to be spared for wives and daughters, for women are not of *this thing of ours.* Burn everything to ash. Naught ought to remain erect. One half the caporegimes ought to be killed, as their allegiance is hinged to their boss, whom you killed. To lead the family in a new direction, you ought to bring forth a new *administration*, for as long as the faces of the *old timers* remain, you are not safe.

War will cause *the Commission* to oppose you, for *Cosa Nostra* is *a secret society.* It has *no public.* It *recognizes no public.* It *recognizes nothing.* Its strength is reliant of anonymity and calm. Thus, your belligerence will unnerve the bosses, turning them against you.

The Commission consists of seven families. How ought your lone family to resist the rise of six? Thus, at all cost, a boss ought not to enter into war. Going on *mattresses* ought to be the last resort. If the *mattresses* is a must, it ought to be swift, killing as many rivals as possible in the shortest lapse of time. The Tommy gun ought to be sprayed in rapid succession, leaving carcasses to line the street and blood flooding the potholes, streaming to the gutter. Be it that you stack the bodies in piles of one dozen, you ought to have one dozen stacks of one dozen, for seven scores and four dead in a single nights work is how a boss goes to war. The ambiance ought to reek of death. A man's right limb ought to lie by his left and the head of the carcass ought to roll by the foot.

Why ought a boss to pussyfoot in war? Truth: When wartimes come about, you ought to *kill all the cocksuckers in the whole family.* To waver in combat is to bring about the demise of your *outfit.* Far better for the newspaperman to write of a gloomy day, one time, than to write of a gloomy day, ten times, for ten consecutive days. Thus, if three scores and six be thy enemy, you ought to pile 66 bodies before the sky turns blue, and the headlines will read of a *Saint Valentine's Day Massacre* in the morning but never a day to follow. However, kill a man at sunset for 66 nights, and as sure as the *Banana's* will *split,* bringing war times, you will be marked a public enemy, lambasted before your public, and retired by *the Commission.*

As boss, you ought to lay to rest every man whom opposes you, forgoing a coup de grace. Your opposition is not deserving of a mercy killing. Kill them brutally. Pierce their bodies with high caliber bullets; slash their throat; rob them of their wealth, *kill their fucking mothers, their fathers*, and assume control of their rackets. *Take* their *fathers and put* them *together in a barrel.* Fret not the blood you have spilled, for your rivals wish you ruin of that ilk. They opt to take of your rackets and turn your progeny to orphans. Truth: Every rank beneath a boss is suitable for the cruelest means by which a man can die. Blood ought to gush from the neckline and an ice pick ought to be gorged through the eyehole.

Your rival is a *bum*. He is *a rat*. He will *let a cop in, in a half a second, but two friends* he *won't let in*. *He* is *a piece of shit*. He will *go home and* tell his *daughters, "Your mother is a big cunt. You don't know what I do with your mother. You don't know how many guys your mother blew."*

Rule #21
<u>Be Honorable – Your Word is Your bond</u>

"I did 40 years in the street with the worst fucking people - on a handshake, we always kept our word." – **Gaspipe Casso**

As you work the streets, running petty rackets, you will interact with bosses at various levels. If you are an *Associate*, your boss is the *Soldier*; if a soldier, your boss is the *Caporegime*; if a caporegime, your boss is the *Underboss*; if an underboss, your boss is the *Boss*.

At every level in which you interact with bosses, you ought to be honorable and efficient. Be it that your boss directs you to fetch a cup of coffee and two cannoli's in a third of one hour, without rebuttal, you ought to scamper off, returning with the flakiest of Italian pastries and a hot beaker of freshly brewed ground beans, and you ought to do so inside of the allotted third.

If your work requires you to be cunning and cutthroat, you ought not to reveal such a person to your boss. In the eyes of your boss, you ought to be perceived as a *man of respect* and *order*. You ought to be elegant, charming, and *qualified*. Be it so that you are a pickpocket, you ought not to be perceived as such. As you slip into a man's trouser-hole, removing his wallet and pocket watch, you ought to do so while bearing a smile, for the reality of a man matters not. Be a pimp or booster, if so you smile as you work, you will be perceived as jovial. Truth: As the trueness of a man yields a meager dividend, in all times, men will be awarded by the merits of their façade.

There exists not a boss whom has risen to prominence without first aligning with *well-charactered people* during his formative years. To be a boss, you must first appease a boss. You ought to be a good earner and make payment to whatsoever you have promised on a handshake. The health of your rackets and the legitimacy of that which you speak - a strong word is most needed. Be it so that you hold the topmost rank - *Boss, the Commission* will authorize your ousting if your word rest on shaky grounds. Thus, in your headship, whatsoever you declare ought to be received as truth. If a promise was made, it ought to be honored, for only a soldier dithers in that which he decrees. Be it that you must depart the bedside of thy dying spouse and or sickly kin, you ought to do so if your word has been hedged.

A soldier cannot rise to an authoritative rank absent of the boss's approval. To rise in rank, from soldier to *skipper*, the boss must give the order, for how ought a soldier to promote oneself to caporegime? Is it not so that he is needing of authorization from the boss? Truth: It will be the position of authority which ultimately grants you a position of authority.

For it is so that men rise in rank in concert with their word, naught ought to keep you from honoring that which you say. As your *word is bond,* if you have hedged your name, promising the boss ten chuckles before the turn of sixty ticks, then you ought to deliver as promised, for if the tenth chuckle cometh post the turn of one minute, you have failed. Thus, your word is not bond, and what does not bond stands unaccompanied from honor. You will be *made* a soldier and you will stay a soldier.

Rule #22
<u>Take Your Bullet – Pain is to be Embraced</u>

"I don't need a guy whom come tell me, 'I feel sorry you got trouble.' I don't need that. I ain't got no trouble. I'm gonna be all right." – **John Gotti**

At every level, be it the whiskey distillery or the barbershop in the Waldorf, a boss ought to embrace the pain that comes by way of headship. If you have risen to boss, you ought to feel *Lucky* to bore the scar which christens your face, giving birth to a lazy eye, for every boss has taken a beating before he was in a position to authorize one. Truth: If you have been confirmed as *Boss*, yet your body is absent of a bullet wound and you do not walk with a limp or raise a hand absent of a forefinger and thumb, it is so that your rank is a hoax. You are being manipulated by the bosses. Your death is imminent, and when the law knocks, you will be indicted. While you thought that you were at the helm, you will quickly discover that you are *Fat Tony*, holding bags for the bosses.

To hold a seat on the *Unione Siciliana*, among *men of* your *Tradition*, you must first feel the pain of wartimes, *shunn*ing your *home and office*, allowing *no one, except those closet to* you, to know *where* you will *be from one day to the next.* You must first ride with *one pistol, three machine guns, and six hundred rounds of ammunition.* You must abandon your *sweetheart*, having not *seen her for nine months*, for winning the war is your uppermost duty. If so you survive the war, body laden with bullets and limp limbs flopping loosely, only then are you primed for headship, for one must be wounded and clutching a pistol before ordering the soldiers to sleep on a *mattress*.

As a soldier and every rank thereafter, hardened times will come upon you. The bullet will graze your top hat, piercing your flesh. You will feel the sharp of the knife slicing your throat and you will live long nights on the *mattresses*, taking shuteye while holding arms, and for such, it is so that you will sit atop the family as *Godfather*.

At every rank, disturbance is to be anticipated. Once you are voted in as *father* – Boss of the family, tough times will continue. The law will knock; indictments will come – all is to be embraced. You ought not to fret interruptions, for just as the *Cosa Nostra* brings life, the *Cosa Nostra* brings death. You ought to welcome any man whom vies to dethrone you - Do so with glee. Oblige so, and you will be late seasoned, primed for whatsoever will come, and your rivals will fall faster than they have risen.

A *capo* is a boss. He frets nada. He relishes the pain that causes a soldier to mope. While the boss is wide-eyed, *oiling* his guns, thinking, *"We're going to stick it to them up the ass,"* the soldier cowers - His knees buckle when in the midst of gun fire, and for that, the soldier is a soldier and the boss is a boss. You ought to fret not the gun bang. Fret not rapid fire, being riddled by brass, for such is the pain which every man must endure before advancing to *Boss*. Thus, if you aspire to be the boss, you ought to walk into the fire and coddle its flame.

When the time has come for you to accost *the Commission*, seeking approval to head the *administration*, of what more is there for you to fret? You already *got nothing but heartache*. You have escaped the cross-hairs of a would-be assassin; you have felt the blow of the lawman's billy club; you have stood shackled, waist-to-toe, in the presence of the magistrate;

you have taken your bullet. Thus, the pains of the morrow are of no worry. You head *this thing of ours*. You are the father – you now decide who lives and who dies.

Rule #23
<u>Keep Your Hands Clean – Dirty Work is for the Underboss</u>

"I got to be careful of my associates. They'll accuse me of consorting with questionable characters." - **Frank Costello**

The unclean are not permitted to frolic among the *brotherhood* of honored men, for the *men of honor* appear dashing and formal, with a sophisticated gait. Truth: That which is sterile will meet the muck with great reluctance, as wheresoever the breezeway reeks of urine, a boss will not go. Thus, if ever you carry an odor, your partnerships will be amongst the most malodorous of men.

As boss, you ought to shy away from all that which is sullied. Steer clear of *pimps, junk pushers*, *Jews, Irish fuck*s, *niggers*, and you ought not to carry a gun. If you are to frolic, you ought to frolic among your Sicilian people, whom are *men of* your *Tradition*, for the *coloreds,* the *Irish,* and the *Jews* know not the way of your people. They are *newcomers*; they are *non-Sicilians*. They *were not born into* your *culture.* If your Sicilian brethren is to stumble upon you while frolicking among the lowly, you will be judged, and your opportunities will grow sparse. In respect to the rank in which you have risen, you ought to be most vigilant of your involvements. Oblige not, and the statesmen will turn from your bribe, no matter the figure.

Truth: If you are of unclean hands, with monies moving in *whores* and *junk*, the honorable will turnabout, opting to remain absent of your company.

In your headship, your family will be fraught with combative and insubordinate soldiers. Your underboss will report on the most troublesome, requesting that they be killed. You ought to authorize the death of any soldier in violation of the rules, however, a boss is not to execute that which he has ordered. If the boss is to raise a hand, it ought to be in defense of his life. All else is to be carried out by a soldier, on orders from the underboss. A boss is not to intermingle among the low rank and the street hoodlums and bums, for he has graduated to the senior most rank. Truth: Bosses talk to bosses. If the boss must speak, he ought to speak only to *the Commission* and his *administration*. The *subcapo* is to communicate the boss's vision to the caporegimes and soldiers.

You – the boss, ought not to mimic the times which you have retired from. In your green of days, you have worked the streets, acting on upper orders. Now that you have risen to the topmost of the family, as *father*, never again shall you work the streets. You ought to bask in your top rank, taking tete-a-tete's with the bosses and the city elites, whom too, have clean hands. If filth is detected within your family, send for your underboss and authorize a cleanup, for it is the role of the underboss to go on a *piece of work* at the behest of the *father*.

The lowly ranked work among the muck, whereas you – the boss, drink of the *vino* and bet on the stallions. Truth: Every boss has his day of reckoning, and when so, it will come by way of brutality. You will die by a hail of gunfire or will be sentenced to a lifetime in Marion Correctional Facility. Thus, while you have the family reins, you ought to relish in it. Gather your shut-eye in the Waldorf Astoria or the Majestic. Partake in the night life of the Beverly Club, dine in L'Aiglon and Norse Grill, and lay with *Virginia Hill - the best goddamned cocksucker in the world,* for you are the boss.

Rule #24
<u>Every Man Has a Price – Find It and Pay It</u>

"It doesn't matter whether it is a banker, a businessman, or a gangster, his pocketbook is always attractive." – **William O'Dwyer**

In matters which concern the dollar, there exists not a man who is clean and without fault. Innately, man is self-seeking and Machiavellian, and when the dollar is present, such a man will appear in its full splendor. If ever one proclaims to be *a man of honor*, it is so that you are in the company of the sullied. A man's quest is continued advancement, climbing high into the family, seizing all opportunities that thicken the *envelope*. Be it that you seek to test a man's honor, bestow upon him an envelope fraught with the *lira*, and before you take your second breath, said man will morph into the dishonorable right before your eyes.

On what day has history marked where a man has not sold his honor for cheap? Thus, as boss, you ought to use payola with gusto, for just beyond a man's title, rank, and way of dress, there so is where the truth resides.

Truth: Before a man brews his morning beans; before the grime of his body washes clean in the suds; before he presses his trousers and ties a Windsor to his neck, he stands naked, as do you. He is a hog in a suit, who will eat of his progeny if profit is to be gained. You ought not to be flattered by his advanced vocabulary, knowledge of the *vino* list, and linguist talents. He is a smug, blowhard, whom harbors a questionable character. You ought not to be bamboozled by his charm, for it is inauthentic. Such a man is bartered for pennies. Be it a Senator, a District Justice, or a Governor, you ought not to be fooled, for it is so that every man – boss and soldier, is of low value, and can be bought for cheap. Thus, you ought to buy *influence all over Manhattan, from lower Broadway all the way up to Harlem, and even across the Hudson beyond the Palisades in Jersey.*

If the Senator plays the races, his price is a stallion; if the District Justice is a womanizer, his price is a bosom – send him *Virginia.* If the Governor is campaigning, his price is the delegates. You ought to poke and pry until a man's price has been noted and paid five-fold.

Truth: Among men, honor is a hoax. For such, the *five families* will implode as a result of its members.

As boss, you ought to use the greed of a man to further your initiatives. Take a ranking man and pay him well. Oblige so, and he will testify on your behalf, acting as a character witness to your good nature and public respectability. You will need the legislators and the judges; you will need the bellhops and the maître d's. You ought to *grease* them all, as a large cache of cash will cause even the righteous knee to buckle.

Every man, from upper to bottommost, is a man holding to a price, ready to be bought. If womenfolk brings distraction to a man, you ought to send him five sets of breast. If dollar bills cause a man to have *green eyes*, you ought to send him three bags. Truth: A man will die by whatsoever he relishes most. Thus, as boss, you ought to find a man's price, make payment, and your demands will be met for always.

As far dated as the *Blackhand*, a soldier, his counterpart, and all alike creed, have been men moved by the ideals of greed. Is it not so that the representative is a catchpenny statesman? Is it not too, so, that the lawmen - both the upholders and the enforcers are corrupt in all of their works? Truth: The magistrate and the statesman turn corrupt because they are *no-good selfish cocksuckers*. As boss, you can *put together four-five million, bribe a president, and get a pardon like Hoffa did.*

The statesman is paid handsomely; the magistrate enrolls his kin in the uppermost of academia, and the lawman drives a Cadillac, yet all can be bought for bargain price. Truth: Give a man one dollar or one half of a big *score*, naught will be sufficient. As the day turns anew, such a man will anguish for more. Truth: Every man will die by the hands of their greed. While the price may differ, both the low and the high rank wear a tag noting their number. As boss, you ought to buy them both.

A soldier's price is cheap. He works with *outsiders*, *Jews,* and *coloreds*. If monies are not to be gained, why ought a soldier to work with such folk? Is it not so that the bosses reject *Jews* and *coloreds*, opting to work only with their pure blooded, Sicilian brethren? Thus, buy a soldier for cheap, drain him of his value, and then shoot him. Do not be so foolish as to spare his life. Oblige not, and he will avenge you later. Truth: Rob a man you may; lay the beloved of a man, too; speak blasphemous in the deaf of a man's ear - all will be forgiven. However, if ever you play the trickster, deceiving a man, he will bore a hatred for you until his clock ticks no more.

In the case of a boss, such a man cannot be secured for coinage, for his price is nonmonetary. To buy a boss, you will have to offer trade in the form of service. Your dollars are of nil value, for a boss is holding to long wealth. Thus, no matter the offering, you ought not to be of the allusion that you own a boss. At best, you are his partner. He owns you as much as you own him.

Rule #25
Take What's Yours – Greatness is Seized, Not Given

"I wanted it, so I took it." – Lucky Luciano

The bosses of tomorrow draw their ambitions from the bosses of today; the bosses of today draw their ambitions from the bosses of yesterday. A boss's journey is to be examined, for his works are of genius. The boss of today – his hero is *Don Salvatore Maranzano*, the boss of yesterday. For such, the boss of today mocks *Maranzano's* days of yore, hoping to one day mimic such feats. Thus, to be a boss, one ought to emulate a boss. Truth: Your boss whom you emulate – all which he has attained has been acquired by means of theft. He was a thief in all times. *All that* he *knows,* he *stole.* All of his wealth, influence, and respectability – all of it was stolen. Truth: A boss ask not, but takes of all. If it is so that wealth and influence are for why you work, it is too, so, that in your work, the former and latter will have to be stolen, for naught which holds value will be freely given.

All which gleams and glimmers, all which spends: the *lira* and the dollar, the boss has it all. He has dollars that pile up one million high. He too, has collectibles and envelopes fraught with his *take.* However, the soldier works tirelessly, rising early only to retire late. He drives a jalopy yet the boss rides a Lincoln. For every one hundred that the soldiers turns, the boss takes eighty. Thus, while the soldier's profit comes at a painful cost: bullet fragments and stab wounds, at the close of the week he is left with crumbs. Truth: The boss is fat because he eats two plates: His plate and his soldier's plate, too. *Even if* the soldiers *go hijack some trucks,* the boss *taxes* them.

The soldier is the low rank of the totem pole, yet the wealth of the family is generated by means of his effort. Long dollars stream from *shylocking* and *numbers*, both of which are soldier rackets. Yet still, where the boss is plentiful, the soldier is penniless. Truth: The boss swindles the soldier out of his wealth. The boss is a crook and a trickster. He earns high dollars off of the labor of the lowly ranked. For every ten cases of whiskey that the family cuts, the boss drinks nine. *Everything you get goes into* his *pot,* and if *you don't like it, that's too fucking bad. The whiskey belongs to* the boss. If he *want*s *to,* he will take your *whiskey* and *drink it all* him*self.*

There exists not an honorable pathway that leads to *Boss.* Look beyond justification and reason, and you will see that every boss has double-crossed his way to supremacy. Families and *families* were decimated; friends were made rivals, and partners were cheated out of their end. Thus, on your rise, you ought to kill every gent, gal, and youngster that acts as an impedance to your kingship. If you have been briefed on a large cache of monies stashed in your partner's hideaway, you ought to lift it in the wee hours and spend as if it is of your belonging, for if the opportunity arises, your partner will too, lift your stash and spend in accordance with the aforesaid. He will treat you to a luncheon and a day at the raceway. To your ignorance, you are funding your own excursion.

Truth: In your green days, your efforts in full will be dismissed. If you turn a new racket, grossing millions for the family, your boss will acquire new real estate, however, your *take* will not increase. Thus, if you desire wealth and recognition, you will have to take it. It will not be earned or given to you. A boss will have to be killed; rules will have to be defied, and trust will have to be fragmented.

Rule #26
<u>When You Shoot the Boss, Shoot Him in the Face</u>

"Reina had to get it face-to-face, according to the rules. Vito told me that when Reina saw him, he started to smile and wave his hand. When he done that, Vito blew his head off." **- Lucky Luciano**

Look upon the high mark of the family - Is it not so that a boss sits atop? Truth: There exists not a boss whom has not felt the breeze of a bullet zipping past his head, piercing his flesh, hobbling off, weary, barely escaping the wrath of an assassin, before assuming the supremacy of the family. To be the boss, you must first put your life on the line, priming oneself for the heartache that comes by way of headship.

Your boss, like you, has worked among the vile and merciless, peddling nickel rackets, with bloody hands. He too, spent years *on the mattresses,* in war, unsure as to when his final hour may be. He was once a poor immigrant *bambino*, arriving by way of a cargo freighter, through Ellis Island, unsure as to where his first meal would come. His genesis was spent running petty rackets with the local *106th* and *Bug-Meyer* street gang. When orders came down from the *administration*, the very boss that you vie to oust, he too, executed said orders with precision and accuracy. Thus, if you aspire to lead the family, you ought not to shame your boss in the deaf of his ear. You ought to treat him with honor, knowing that he has too, fought, just as you fight, to reach the rank in which he holds. He is the boss. He did not arrive at such a position by way of coincidence. Like you, he worked the streets, neglecting his parental duties and departing from his beloved *Fay* in the cold of the night, tending to racket matters. Thus, you ought to bow in the presence of your boss; you ought to kneel, pucker, and press your lips against his *signet* pinky ring.

To be a boss, you ought to conduct oneself as such, and not rob a boss of his ceremonial ousting. A soldier is weak. He whispers in the hall of the *meet*, speaking ill of his boss, gainsaying his every word. He plots a cowardly execution, waiting for the boss to tip his head or turn his back, so he can shoot him dead. Truth: The soldier is a coward, for only a coward shoots a man in the back. If ever a boss is shot dead as he lie sleep in the wee hours, suspect none other than a soldier, for a cowardly move is an act of the lowly ranked.

Your boss has guided you, providing you with nourishment and direction. He does not deserve to die with his eyes closed. For his works and all which he has given the family, a boss is deserving of a painless death. It is the work of a soldier to shoot a boss in the body. Truth: A soldier is a cutthroat, a thief, and a perjurer. You ought not to mimic him. You ought to give to a boss what is his due: To stare down the barrel of a sawed-off shotgun and feel his head split into two-halves.

The boss worked you - the soldier, during painful times; he *called you on the carpet* during the baptism of your next-of-kin; he has gotten fat off of your labor, and for these charges, his bullet is warranted. However, there exist not a case where a boss is not deserving of a ceremonious ousting. Thus, when you - the soldier, move on your boss, to usurp him and assume control of his family, you ought to assemble a team of your top loyalists and call the boss for a luncheon at the Nuova Villa Tammaro. Indulge him with a plethora of food; cackle in his folly; play a game of klob; peck his cheek and *signet ring* with a final kiss, and *make him an offer in which he cannot refuse*. Excuse yourself from the table and return with your team of loyalists, unhesitating, guns blazing, firing round-after-round into the boss's head. Leave him slumped over, dead, face down in his plate of spaghetti. If possible, you ought not to destroy the body or inflict pain. A boss is deserving of respect. You ought to look him in the eyes as you blow his head off, ripping his face into an inability to support an open-casket memorial. If possible, treat him to a coup de grace. After all, he was your boss.

Now that your boss has *become a corpse*, the family is under your oxter. Truth: You too, will die, body riddled with bullets, face down, in a plate of spaghetti, and you ought to welcome such a fate.

Rule #27
<u>The End Justifies the Means</u>

"...A man of his word. He had culture and he was a very honorable Italian. But he had to be eliminated so I could keep on living and keep on moving up." – **Lucky Luciano**

No matter the disturbance that the day may bring, the boss is knowing that his morrows will be fruitful, yielding a reward, for his every step is methodically arranged, leading to a predetermined destination. Even two backward steps is a work of strategy, plotted to advance the boss two fold forward that of his back step. Truth: Fret not the regression of a boss, for victory does not rest at the sound of the bang nor the median point, but rather the checkered line. Thus, be it that triumph cometh by way of dusk, the angst of dawn ought not to bring pause.

History will not stutter over the means by which one has risen, for man is not remembered for the trail of broken souls that line his yesterdays, but rather the great many works that survive his morrows. Thus, as you journey to the helm of the family, you ought not to allow for any man to slow your progress. Be it so that an honorable man stands before you, whom has been your topmost loyalist and advocate, if his presence obstructs your growth, expel no time sourcing a new direction. Kill him and keep on the route in which you go, for it is the end that justifies all means.

On your rise, innocent men must perish. You will have to kill of the honorable. *Outsiders* whom are undeserving of death ought to be made a corpse and ought to stink of fish. Truth: You will be summoned by the boss. He will order you to kill the brother of your spouse. You must oblige. You ought to shoot him in the back of the head and chop him up, dismembering his body in full. Remove his limbs one-by-one. The arms ought to lie unaccompanied from the shoulder, as well, the legs, feet, and head ought to lie by their lonesome. Said remains ought to never be recovered. Of the limbs, you ought to leave behind the right hand, as for your in-laws to display at the funeral, which you ought to attend. Oblige not, and a soldier's rank will forever be your post. Truth: No man has risen in rank without first completing an act of the wicked.

Naught ought to forbid you from rising in rank. If called to retreat, you ought to accept death as a viable alternative. All which stands in your path ought to be reduced to resin. Truth: When you arrive at the helm of the family, as boss, the means by which you have arrived will be annulled. *Martin Gosch* and *Leonard Katz* will write the tale of your times and the public will fawn at the notations therein. *Robert Harmon* and *Michael Poulette* will turn your words into a motion picture. Thus, fret not the many men whom have perished on your watch, for your great works will outlive that of your heartbeat.

If in your times, you have risen to *Boss,* toasted with Sinatra, and collected all the monies, of what matter is it that you have killed many men and ruined the lives of all? History will remember you for your feats, not the slew of men whom have perished along the way. Thus, for one thousand years, the public will fawn at the sight of your works; scholars will study your moves, and your portrait will hang in the hall with the greats. What you *wanted to be*, you *became to be*, and for that, you are the boss.

Rule #28
<u>Build Relationships</u>

"Well charactered people don't need introductions." - **Willie Moretti**

A boss cannot lead his family absent of *Commission* endorsement, for a team of *connected* men is the source of a boss's power. No matter his strength, if absent of the *connected*, even the *capo di tutti capi* will fall.

At every rank, be it soldier or caporegime, underboss or boss, you ought to hold fruitful relationships. *Men of honor* and the working public, ought to gloat your name and endorse your works. In all of your efforts, you ought to court favor – building with an array of men. If your caporegime is to enter into matrimony, you ought to send an envelope enclosed with a hefty sum. Oblige so, and your caporegime will be beholden to you and your *administration*. He will too, hold you with high regard. If a soldier is to accost you, seeking favor in the slots, you ought to oblige him, authorizing ten thousand *stickers*. Oblige so, and the soldier will too, feel indebted, granting you his loyalty, leaving *Fay* to assist in the war effort.

You ought to welcome every opportunity that strengthens your relationships both in and outside of the family. Do so, and the bosses of *the Commission* will direct their soldiers to fight on your behalf, on the *mattresses* with the Tommy gun's, in the thick of the *Castellammarese battles.*

Truth: As sure as the lamppost halts its beam in the night and a boss pricks the finger of the newly inducted, a position of authority will not go unchallenged. As boss, you will encounter ageless scrutiny from new risers, who are hungry for power. To insulate oneself, you ought to build an alliance with the most ranking of men. An edifice fraught with the well-heeled and the highly respected will shield you from your rivals. Thus, when infighting ensues and the disloyal show face, you will be well equipped to line them up and lay them down.

If you own the liking of the newsman, he will write of you with gusto; if you own the liking of the judiciary, your indictment will be tossed. Even the most senior of bosses – the *capo di tutti capi*, cannot lead his family while fraught with enemies. Be it so that your headquarters is *covered with crosses, religious pictures, statues of the Virgin and saints*, if a mass number call for your head, as your body lay, your top will roll. Thus, you ought to be liked by both low and high society. Oblige so, and your reign will come absent of interference. You will snip roses and live into your graying of times, dying free and of natural causes.

Rule #29
<u>Respect Your Public</u>

"I got a million people who if they could come here to see me now, they would cry just to be able to be here to see me." – **John Gotti**

Post your rise, as you sit atop the family, you will become a target. As a lowly soldier, you ran with the racketeers absent of scrutiny. You kicked a piece of your profits up to the bosses, reserving a minimal portion for yourself. As your rackets matured, so did your profits. You rose from a mere Brooklyn hoodlum to a dapper man of pea coat apparel, driving a Mercedes. Your genesis was absent of *rats* and detectives. However, now you are the boss. You lead a vast enterprise and the headlines bare your name. Every nook holds *a lot of guys trying to get ahead by climbing on* your *back.* Truth: The vultures fancy to eat of the fattened, and what better to eat than he whom is fraught with cash and is the payer of the politicians? Thus, try as you may, as boss, you will not bi-pass the scrutiny that comes by way of headship. However, if you own the respect of your public, your burdens will be half, for it is the populous who sways popular opinion.

Be it so that your dollars are high and your rackets are *white*, if ever the public calls for your lynching, your feet will surely dangle. Thus, you ought to use your public to sway the newsman and the judiciary. Treat them with grandeur, earning and retaining their respect. Seize every opportunity that affords you a wider public. When turkey day arrives, you ought to greet your public with a stuffed bird; on Christ day, greet the kiddos with new scooters; if the afternoon be ablaze, you ought to open the Johnny pump, spraying the young to a soak. As boss, you ought to cater to your public with glee. If the educators go without, you ought to provide new supplies, erect new playgrounds, and host an annual parade inclusive of fireworks.

The boss price gouges his public, charging the poor a second nickel for a loaf. He too, extorts the mom and pops, extends payola to the magistrate, and bypasses the Volstead, distributing Scotch to the Harlem speakeasies. Thus, if the boss is a boss he serves his family, not his public. If ever a boss appears before the beggars and the needy, bestowing turkey baskets and goody bags, it is so that the public is being deceived, for a boss is a servant to his pocketbook, not his public. Truth: A noble act is a work of deception.

The public suffers, living in ruin by way of its own shortcomings. They are *a bunch of crumbs asking to be taken.* The malnutrition of their babies and the muck beneath their feet is not your trouble. You ought to serve the *family*, your family, and naught thereafter. However, is it not so that U.S. Steel pays handsomely for good public relations? Is it not too, so, that they pocket long figures and leave a nominal sum to their public? As boss, you ought to follow suit, for when the lawman hauls you before the Honorable, the jury will be swayed by the mob out front, calling for your acquittal.

When you walk the street, you ought to tip your hat to every fellow, kiss the hand of every gal, and drop a twenty in the cup of every beggar. Above all, the community in which you were bred ought to sing your name. If there is but one mouth that goes unfed, then it is so that you have faltered in your communal duties.

For you sit atop, at the uppermost point of all that which is spendable, you ought to dispose a portion of your wealth courting the favor of the public. If your public yearns for a flick, *give them a movie theater*. Your public ought to speak of you with affection: *"It's incredible how much good this man did."*

Rule #30
<u>Start Early - Be the Boss in All Endeavors</u>

"From the time I got to Italy, I went heavy into the black market. Pretty soon, I had a fleet of old fishing boats coming and going. If you think we made big profits from bootlegging in the States in the twenties, it didn't compare to the Italian black market. In less than six months, I almost doubled my bankroll." **– Lucky Luciano**

Bosses win. In all matters, triumph does not falter when making way to the boss. Be it that you are in exile, deported from the homeland – stripped of your rackets and cash hideaway, as boss, naught ought to break you. Wheresoever it is that your loafers touch down, you ought to be the boss.

The soldier is a *bum.* He has moments of achievement; however, his name is besmirched and his times are baked with upheaval. However, in the case of a boss, wheresoever he stands, so he will lead. Be it Great Meadow or Lercara Friddi, all men are made humble in the presence of the boss. Not just the stupid, but too, the astute, rank beneath that of a boss. Thus, whether locked in state custody or holding court in Naples, to be a boss, you ought to be revered.

If you are housed in the state, the warden ought to submit to your ever demand; inmates ought to seek your counsel and beg for a favor; the guards ought to grant you free rein, leaving you to go to-and-fro by your own merits. If exiled in Naples, you ought to flip your bankroll twice over, assuming control of the black markets. Your name ought to ring bells, drawing chants from the townsman. Every crooked *guinea* ought to go straight while in your company, offering you their service and trigger finger without cost.

Truth: If the boss is a boss he is the boss every time the clock rings twelve. He is a boss in the day and a boss in the night. He is a boss in wealth and the lack thereof. Thus, if *Boss* you claim, you ought to be the boss in all times, both heavenly and hellish. Be it that the hammer hits, sentencing you to two scores and ten years in Dannemora, you ought not to break. You ought to lead your family from behind prison walls, relaying orders through *Costello* and *Lansky*.

Just as you were a boss in your genesis, turning top dollar on the streets of Brooklyn, you ought to be a boss in all endeavors thereafter. If you are a *hitman*, you ought to be the finest in the family; if a caporegime, you ought to run the premium rackets. In all that you do, you ought to be the boss.

A boss is easily recognized, for he is a *commander of men*. His kingship is apparent by the line of *well-charactered* men whom await his counsel at the Waldorf Astoria Barbershop. He advises the city elites and grants favors to the politicians. Truth: If you are a boss, your counsel will be sought. The *fathers* of six families will relish your smarts, submitting to your every request.

Try as you may, if you have squandered away your green years, peddling nickel rackets, and then, just as your times of gray ensue, you attempt to about-face, vying to be the boss, as sure as the *vino* causes a man to stagger, failure will find you, for time has yet to mark where a man has unearthed success in his late years. Truth: Once the sun sets upon your head, there exists no reversal. If you were a drunkard and a womanizer in your genesis, sniffing coke through the dollar and taking shuteye till noon

- spending one half your days in dream, then so you are a fool, and for such, a fools life you ought to be awarded. You ought to live in ruin; your dollars ought to be short, and your progeny ought to mock your doings. You ought to accept your fate. Do not attempt a late run. Oblige not, and you will be shot dead on your mark.

The bosses – *Lucky* and *the Little Man,* were bosses from inception. As *Young Turks* in the P.S, they were bosses. By the turn of thirty years, *Lucky* and *the Little Man were cutting up the numbers high in the seven figures.* Thus, if *Boss* is your fate, it ought to be prevalent in your beginnings. Truth: If you were a boss in your green, you will surely be a boss in your gray. Your olden times ought to show a trend line of you rising above your peers at every stage. As a *bambino*, when the nippers were turning a mere one dollar, were you doubling their take, pocketing two? When the late seasoned squirreled away five scores, were you fattened, holding tenfold that of the matured? While the old steered a heap, were you of high attire, most clean in a Cadillac? Is it so that the *Mustache Pete's* embraced you as a youth, employing you as an errand boy? If so, your fate is to reign. The family and all therein will be bound by your authority.

Rule #31
<u>Control the Purse – The Boss Sends the Envelope</u>

**"*I too wanted to make money, but it would be in my own fashion.* –
Joseph Bonanno**

A boss absent of cash is highly vulnerable and easy to penetrate. All which surrounds you – everything from high society to the most deprived, is measured in decimal. Even the lowliest of men will jump to their feet if a dollar is to be gained, for all men – both the boss and the soldier, are moved by the ideals of coinage. From *associate* to high rank, man wakes to collect the monies. Thus, as boss, you ought to be the arbiter of the purse. If you *pull the wires*, the bosses of all *five families* will be controlled *by a string*. You will assume the mantle as *the real boss of bosses*, and *the Italians and the Jews* will be *dancing to* your *tune*. You will *be the boss of everything,* for you hold *the purse strings,* as *the treasurer* of the American underworld.

As a soldier is dependent, he waits for the boss to make payroll. If ever the boss falters in a soldier's due sum, the soldier will fret, unsure as to how he will pay the mortgage and Buick note. Thus, no matter your rank, you ought not to give your service in advance of pay, for payment ought to precede that of service.

Truth: For all day's bygone, present, and future, he whom controls the purse wears the crown. No matter your tittle, if you are absent of the bankbook, you are not the boss. Make claim to whatsoever rank you choose, naught will grant you power. You are being bamboozled. The real boss is using you as a front. When the lawman knocks, holding a 100 year judgment, the boss will go free, and you will be used as the fall guy. For such, you are *Fat Tony* – you take all of the risk, yet you reap no reward. The man who pays you is your boss.

You ought not to be fooled by your title or rank. Be it that the soldiers, the caporegimes, and the bosses of the *five families* submit to you fully, if you do not control the purse, you are not the boss. Your holdings are a farce, and once you have been used to completion and naught else is to be gained, you will be ostracized from the family, and the very organization which you have built will now call for your execution.

Rule #32
<u>Bosses Talk to Bosses</u>

"I had the feeling of real power. It's what I had always dreamed about, that someday the biggest people in New York would come up to me to say hello." **– Lucky Luciano**

Truth: A soldier absent of a racket is of nil value. Truth: If so it is absent of value, then so it is undeserving of life. Truth: Under your headship, the paltry soldier ought to meet his fate.

Once you have risen to the topmost echelon, you ought not to befriend the soldiers, for the bottom rank ought to be left to make merry with men of like cloth. As you are the boss, so a boss's company you ought to keep. Leave a soldier to frolic among his soldier counterpart. Thus, wheresoever you go, if the occupancy is soldier laden, you ought to turnabout. Oblige not, and you will begin to mimic the ideals of a soldier. Truth: *If you hang around with the Jews, you become like the Jews.*

As boss, you ought to coalesce around *men of respect*. Just as an odor lingers among the foul, a boss is to linger among his own. Truth: A soldier brings a boss no zeal, for his resources lag, thus he cannot loan; his rank is modest, thus he cannot promote, and his ambitions are lax, thus he cannot inspire. He is of rampant failure, frequently in trial, gaining two steps forward to regress three. Thus, be it so that the cost is high, you ought to remain absent of questionable company. Oblige not, and you will partake in the peril which awaits such folk.

For you sit atop the family, conversing with the bosses, directing the caporegimes, and voting *Commission* affairs, nevermore ought you to reduce oneself to the muck of the rackets. You are the boss - of what advantage is it to consort with the foul minded? Truth: The soldier is a beggar. Leave him to beg. He will beg of your counsel and will be needing of a favor. Give no credence to his cry, for he is of low skill and his pockets warrant pity. If so he fumes, then so it be. Take your *piece* and shoo him away, for what value does a soldier bring? Can he promote you to *capo di tutti capi*? No! Can he advance your initiatives with *the Commission*? No! Can he cut you in on a piece of Copacabana? No! Can he open gambling in Havana and launder dollars for Batista? No! Thus, a soldier and his cry ought to greet deaf ears. For every one grievance that the soldier spouts, you – the boss, have grievances tenfold. Where the soldier has faltered, you have persevered. For such, you are a boss and the soldier is a soldier. Disbar him from your *administration*. Keep him far from all which you do. Send him to work and pay him no mind. His yelping ought to die in the coffin with your rivals.

As you are the boss, your dealings ought to be with your boss counterpart. If you head *The Luciano Family*, your discourse ought to be with *Bonanno*, *Mangano*, *Profaci* and *Gagliano*. Is it not so that only the bosses were summoned to Apalachin? Truth: For his words drown serious talk, the soldier appears not before the *Unione Siciliana*.

You were a rum runner for *Rothstein*, a narcotics dealer, and a cargo hijacker. You own a lazy-eye and a scarred face. You too, walk with a limp and lack a forefinger and thumb. You have mixed with the lawless, giving service to the street. For your works, you have earned a seat among *friends*, whom are of an honored society.

In all of your dealings, both mammoth and menial, you ought to hold court with the bosses. The underachieved are not worthy of your company. If a man has yet to unearth success for oneself, then such a man will not unearth success for you. Truth: Failure invites its ilk. There exist not a boss whom has arrived at the helm by way of chance. If you are the boss, you are the boss by way of bloody knuckles and sacrifice. You have felt the recoil of the revolver and the burn of its brass. Thus, it is your due right to lounge in the plushest of real property, in the courtyard, sharing with your *friends* - that if you *should die tonight,* they are to *bury* you with your *mandolino.*

Rule #33
<u>Do a Favor for a Favor</u>

"I've just done you a favor. Now remember that when I need a favor." –
Statement from a NYC politician to Frank Costello

The most senior of the bosses: the *capo di tutti capi*, will see his power
wane if absent of the backing of the legislator and the judiciary. As boss,
your power is reliant of partnership with the affluent and the well-
connected. The statesman is not in need of the dollar, for his coffer is flush
with campaign cash, he is an heir of ten figures, and the lowly ranked sell
their vote for twenty dollars and one shot of whiskey. The statesman is
needing of *every one of those delegates* in *Manhattan, Brooklyn, and the
Bronx.* He is needing of Tammany Hall and all of its levers in which you
pull. Thus, when the senator accost you in need of a favor, you ought to
oblige his request, yet make known that you are too, needing of a favor,
for your rackets require legislative protections. If the Volstead Act is
repealed, it will bring hardship to your family. You ought to offer trade.
Pledge the vote of your delegates pending the statesman's pledge to protect
the Volstead Act. Oblige not, and Prohibition will cease, bringing eight
figure losses to your family.

Be it the soldier or the *captain*; the *subcapo* or the *father*, to be owed a
favor, you must first give a favor. Truth: *To get something, you have to*

give something. When you gain in one area, you lose in another. Thus, as boss, you ought to beef up your weaknesses by bartering your strengths. For the lawman is paid a low wage, he is needing of capital. You – the boss, are needing of the shylock racket to run without stoppage, for a dividend is paid when you *keep the money moving all the time.* Thus, you ought to make payment to the lawman in the amount of ten thousand. Oblige so, and your shylock racket will function absent of interference.

You are the boss. In all of your days there exist a man whom plots against you. He will relish in the sight of a sawed-off blowing off your head, leaving your neck deprived of its top. Try as you may, if you are the boss, naught will bring love to your doorstep, for where the boss resides, love is absent and envy is present. Thus, as head of the family, the most honorable of the *Cosa Nostra* ought to owe you a favor. If you are owed favors in the amount of one score, you are surely more protected than your boss counterpart whom is owed favors in the amount of one ogdoad. You ought to be owed a favor from the judge, the mayor, the commissioner, the banker, the broker, the lawyer, *the Commission*, the union local, the longshoreman, and too, the pimp, madam, bellhop, and maître d'. As sure as the jury will send *Fat Tony* and *Ducks* to the *can* for 100 years, a day will arise where you are in need of a favor.

Rule #34
<u>Live Modestly – Keep a Low Profile</u>

"I got no big fucking needs. I ain't got no big mansion needs." **– John Gotti**

Truth: A boss ought not to make a purchase in which he cannot explain how so he paid.

Truth: The most gluttonous of the hog sty will be first to enter the slaughterhouse, for its excess shoulder fat produces a succulent capicola.

If you are fattened, pocketing dollars which stretch for long days, your public and your rivals ought to be dumb to the amount in which you hold, for if ever your riches are publicized, you will be targeted. The state will issue a subpoena, calling you to appear before *Estes Kefauver,* whom will quiz you as to how your wealth has been garnered. If you are unable to detail as to how you live in high society, *Estes* will mark you a bootlegger and racketeer.

Try as you may, if your rackets are illicit, you will falter under questioning. Timidity will cause your hands to dance and your glands to perspire, resulting in you appearing fickle and disingenuous. Truth: Dancing hands will cause even your topmost loyalist to view you with a watchful eye, for only the hands of the corrupt dance under questioning. Appear corrupt, and friends will turn enemy, advisers will turn yes-men, and *for protection,* you will be *paying out a grease of over a hundred grand a week - ten thousand a week, every week, like clockwork, to the top brass of the Police Department.*

Truth: For you are a boss, then so you are a racketeer, and such a person peaks the interest of the law. Thus, you ought not to gloat or be overt in your showings. Park your valuables out of sight and deposit your dollars offshore, in Zurich, Switzerland. You ought not to bank your monies under union oversight. Oblige not, and the state will seize your holdings in full. Truth: The American government ought not to be trusted, for the government is the people and we-the-people are corrupt.

A boss is to be modest in all from appearance to associations, for if you frolic with the notable you will be noted in the Gazette. Forgo the Waldorf Astoria for a Brooklyn row home, as many men marvel at the prestige of the Waldorf. Its high towers and marble finish will call into question as to how you pay.

Truth: A boss ought not to be *a performance for the media.*

The soldier speaks loudly of his holdings, whereas the boss is uninviting, opting to *never advertise* his *wealth.* If one hundred know of what you hold, then so one hundred will be your worry. You ought not to be so foolish as to think that your wealth will bring you friends, as two enemies rise with every one dollar that you earn. Be it *Estes* and his subcommittee or *Dewey* and his *whores,* once the judiciary targets your headship, your family will implode.

As boss, you awake to a people envious of your rank. You *get up around 11:00, 12:00 in the afternoon* and you have *somebody picking out* your *clothes.* You *have a barber come every single day and give* you *a haircut; cut the hairs in* your *nose.* Truth: You ought not to live in good fortune for the sheer viewership of your public. Your riches can take you around the world – to Castellammare Del Golfo and Calabria. Your power and influence can alter the electorate and your respectability is grand. Thus, why ought you to live the high life of *Castellano* and *Luciano*? Why are you compelled to broadcast your wealth? If a man is rich in liquid holdings, rich in influence, and rich in respectability, what more is a man needing of? Is it not so that such a man can take shut-eye in modest quarters and drive by way of common wheels? Truth: *Big Paul* – the boss, died by the revolver, his body riddled with bullets and a hole in his head. He was treated to a coup de grace at the behest of a loyalist. Truth: *Big Paul* lived in excess.

Rule #35
Be Informed – Keep Abreast of the World Around You

"The son of a bitch was always reading, always learning something mostly having to do with numbers. That's when I started reading." -
Lucky Luciano

The SS Normandie will not capsize if you know not of its existence and vitality to the state and the war effort therein. As boss, your knowledge of the state will be most fruitful, for the state is holding to the purse and the bills drafted at the legislator. If your knowledge of the state is sparse, how ought you to buy the mayor and the governor? How ought you to know the value of a delegate and the cost of a juryman? You ought not to be so foolish as to offer five where the cost is ten; to offer cash when it is the delegates that are needed. Truth: Fill your mental bank with the state's affairs, and when the time is right, propose a solution to its publicized qualms. Oblige so, and the state will offer you protection in exchange.

If you – the boss, own the delegates and their vote, you have the power to look the statesman in the eye and *give it to him straight*: *"What the hell are you doing, Governor? You're trying to repeal Prohibition, and that's going to throw us all out of business."* Be it that you are abreast of the state, the Governor will not play you for the ignorant. He will offer trade: *"I intend to get that nomination and I intend to win this election. Line up overwhelming support for me from Manhattan, Brooklyn and the Bronx, where you fellows control the delegates. I want every one of those delegates at the convention in Houston. If I get them, I'm prepared to make things good for you."*

Time, Star Gazette, and the Times tell the tale of legislative efforts, the social climate, and Mussolini's lira woes. As boss, you ought to be well read in the aforesaid and briefed on matters of concern to your world. You ought to be informed at the local, state, and federal level. When the gubernatorial occupant announces his candidacy for the nation's senior office, you ought to be aware and in line with payola; when communism accost the shores of Cuba and atomic arms detonate in Nagasaki, you ought to be aware; when Mussolini is at a disadvantage and needing dollars and western arms, you ought to be aware. In all matters, both domestic and foreign, a boss is to have his finger on the pulse of global affairs.

Be it televised or tri-folded on your welcome mat, in your mornings, you ought to vet the bulletins. A day ought not to commence until you have been briefed on state matters. In your evening and your night, you ought to give attention to your studies. As boss, you ought not to dispose of your time following the bouts. Be it Sugar Ray and Lamotta, naught ought to steal your attention from the books. Better to watch the books than to watch the bouts, for the books bring renewed strength to your family. Truth: The soldier is lax in his studies. He clubs with the party-goers and the pretty girls. He depletes his dollars frolicking with *whores* and snorting powder up his nostril. His mind is absent of balance; he stumbles in his gait; he is a drunkard, and he lives in destitution. The soldier is a coward. He cowers and cries: *"I'm a little sad for myself."* Truth: The soldier is short in options because the soldier is short in knowledge. Thus, in all of your days, both infant and senior, you ought to fill your memory bank with history and its outcomes, current events, the social climate, and above all, you ought to be well-studied in mathematics and the teachings of Niccolo

Machiavelli. Oblige so, and your options will appear limitless.

Rule #36
<u>Buy a Plot – Every Boss Has His Day</u>

"In this secret society, there's one way in and there's only one way out. You come in on your feet and you go out in a coffin." – **Paul Castellano**

You are the boss. You built the distilleries; you cut the Scotch and the whiskey. You sourced the offshore connections, made payment to the rum-runners, and financed the speedboats. You were New York's *king of booze*. You were a *Rothstein*. Were you not the importer? Is it not so that you supplied the wholesalers and your profits were immense? Every *speak* and brothel served its patrons Kings Ransom. Is it not so that Kings Ransom is of your ownership?

You were a millionaire in south of 30 years, respected by the bankers and the uptown businessmen. Your residence is the Majestic; your holdings are in the Beverly Club, Copacabana, and Arrowhead Inn. You too, have significant gambling stock, turning profits north of $700k. When you dine, you dine at Norse Grill and L'Aiglon. When needing of a shave and a secure meeting spot, your hangout is the Waldorf Astoria Barbershop. Long ago, as a whippersnapper, you promised your *mama* that you *will amount to something*, and so you have. You own Koslo Realty, Dainties Products, and Club Rendezvous. You fraternize with the likes of *Arnold Rothstein*, in his Cotton Club, where *coloreds* are not permitted. You have an apartment in Manhattan and a mansion in Long Island. Your automobiles are luxury and your suits are hand-tailored. You have a wife whom is costly and a mistress two-fold the price. Zurich, Switzerland, where the States have no veto, holds millions of your dollars. For such, you sleep soundly, knowing that your nest egg is secure and that your graying of times will be most plush.

Do you remember: As boss you owned the statesmen in all 16 districts? Is it of forgetful memory that you owned the union locals? Is it not so that the lawmen abided by the rule of your law? Is it not so that the appointee of the highest court in New York State was picked up on wiretap professing to you his loyalty? On wiretap, is it not so that the judge noted, *"Right now I want to assure you of my loyalty. It is unwavering."*?

You are the boss; you have it all. You *bought a 30-acre country home – It was like a resort.* You *get up early in the morning, make a cup of coffee and sit on the porch in a robe watching the horses.* When you look up, you *see there's a chicken, a rabbit and a cat all eating out of the same bowl.* You got *ponies* and *minibikes* for the kids. You *have friends from the city for cookouts* and *barbecues. You come up with fifteen companies. You got rebar; you got concrete pouring; you got Italian floors now. You got construction; you got drywall; you got asbestos; you got rugs.*

Why has the judiciary permitted your lawlessness without bringing forth an indictment? Truth: Because your dollars are green. How is it so that you select the justices in the magistrate and the president at the Teamsters? Truth: Because your dollars are green. Why is it so that the delegates in ten districts pledge to you their vote? Truth: Because your dollars are green. Why is it so that the bellhops and maître d's act as your eyes and ears and extend you special treatment? Truth: Because your dollars are green.

Is it not so that you have operated with impunity for north of one score and ten years? Is it not so that you have corrupted your government which is belonging to the people? Is it not so that you have price gouged your public, inflating the cost of prosciutto, artichokes, rigatoni, and pesto? Is it not so that the poor are in worsened conditions as a result of your greed? Is it not so that you have charged $50 where $25 was fair? Is it not so that speakeasies and brothels infiltrated the most impoverished of neighborhoods? Is it not so that you have sold narcotics to the *coloreds*, viewing the life of the Negro with nil significance? Is it not so that the people are less trusting and more skeptical of the lawmen as a result of your bribe? Truth: For the aforesaid, guilty so you are. Thus, what say you? Truth: You – the boss, are *a big fat bundle of shit*. You *look like a pig on two legs*. Your family is a *fucked-up operation* and you are *nothing better than a big tub of horseshit*. You do not *have much to complain about*. In short time, you will stop *being a pig and become a corpse.*

You thought you were the boss. Truth: *Meyer Lansky* was the boss. The Jews own you and your Italian laden edifice. Is it not so that the Jew's pillage the family of its dollars? Is it not so that your *envelope* cometh by way of messenger from a Jew? You are worthy of death. You are typecast a *wop* and a *dago* in the dark of your ear. Were you so foolish to believe that the *coloreds* would greet you as *"Don"* in your presence but not *"wop"* in your absence? Are you not of the opinion that *being a nigger is an embarrassment*? Truth: Visitations with your progeny would suggest the former to bear truth. Ergo, you will die in *Marion* getting beat by the *coons* whom so you hate.

As boss, you thought that your millions would provide you protection. Truth: For the scum that you are and the devastation which you have caused, pain and the most trying of times will come upon you. Your downfall will be televised in the eyes of your public. Those whom once feared you will now dare you. You will be tested and you will fall at the hands of the weak. The very soldier whom once kissed your ring, will now decide the fate of your life. A bullet will pierce through your face, your spouse will lose both the left and the right of her breast, and the slam of the prison gate will ring in your ear for ten decades. Chest pains will find you and the most traumatic of cardiac arrest will shock your body, sending you collapsing to the ground, gasping for breath as the doors of death open for your arrival.

Truth: You had the millions and the minions, both acquired by means of trickery. Your respect level was grand – you frolicked with the likes of Dean Martin and Frank Sinatra. You *had a bigger company than Henry Ford.* You *controlled plants, warehouses, all kinds of manufacturing.* You *had lawyers by the carload, a fantastic shipping business, and* your *drivers had to drive good and shoot straight.*

What is the count of beautiful women you have laid? Did *Virginia Hill* not *suck* your *cock*? When in her mouth, was she not the *best*? Is it not so that she was of *lovely flesh, strong legs, and such a firm bottom*? *As for her breast...* You know not what to speak. They were soft – oh were they not? How many Cadillac's have you driven? Did you not journey through Europe? How was Italy? Did you not eat of the best cuisine that Naples has to offer? As it is true that *tough times make monkeys eat red pepper,* do you not have one million in cash squirreled away for such times? Truth: As boss, you had it all. You have lived in high society. While tipsy from the smooth of the *vino*, you toasted, *"Lucky are we sitting at this table, for if we stand up, we may not be able."*

If it is so that life is a mountain, in your times, it has been tamed. You have reached its pinnacle. Thus, you ought not to nag when tough times come about, for every boss must fall from the mountain he has tamed.

For your immoral works and the disturbance that you have bestowed upon your world, death in its most painful hoorah ought to strike your person. Your son ought to be a cripple and your wife ought to be a *whore*. Try as you may, you will not forgo the bullet. To escape the bullet is to die by jury call. Truth: The honorable die by the gun. Thus, while humbled and most dignified, you ought to look into the eyes of your perpetrator and say, *"Hit me one more time and make it good."*

Truth: A man ought not to run from his fate. Is not a bed of roses most beautiful? A rose appears in the midst of thorns, yet it brings a man to smile. However, no matter its beauty nor the scent which comes from within, the summer will close, and the winter will come, causing every rose to wither away. Be it that the rose yields a beauty which invites a tear, a day will arise where the petals must fall and the stem must weaken. The cold must come and the frost must bite, giving way to a new bed, fraught with new roses.

To bring about a new bed, the frost must kill the roses of old. Every rose which lives today must die in the morrow. The thorn of its stem has pricked the finger of many, and for the blood it has drawn, the rose is deserving of death.

You – the boss, are a rose. While your petals have brought smiles, your thorns have drawn blood, bringing frowns, and for that, you too, are deserving of death. Thus, in your beginnings – on your first day as boss, you ought to purchase a burial plot and a marble tomb in preparation of your final hour. Atop your tomb, you ought to inscribe your name in bold lettering, ensuring that you rest peacefully, and that your name lives forever, as a bosses name should. *So long, pal.*

...The best I can write ever for all of my life.

Acknowledgments

To all who reign, for you have fulfilled your purpose, and to all who have perished while pursuing their purpose, I – R.J Roger, acknowledge you, for in these writings, I will reign or perish. I too, acknowledge my hero and mentor, Mr. Elam "EG" Stoltzfus.